MELANCHOLIA
ABUSE                    R-
DENT S                    S
REVERSAL OF
FORTUNE BAD
TREATMENT
BY RELATIVES
JEALOUSY
PRIDE RELIGION
SEDUCTION
LOVE AND DIS-
APPOINTED
AFFECTIONS

# ASYLUM

Brendan Kelly

INSIDE
GRANGEGORMAN

Acadamh Ríoga na hÉireann
Royal Irish Academy

Asylum: Inside Grangegorman

First published 2023
Royal Irish Academy, 19 Dawson Street, Dublin 2
ria.ie

ISBN 978-1-911479-29-1 (pb)
ISBN 978-1-911479-30-7 (pdf)
ISBN 978-1-911479-31-4 (epub)

British Library Cataloguing in Publication Data. A CIP catalogue record for this book is available from the British Library.

Book design and illustration: Fidelma Slattery
Copyeditor: Maggie Armstrong
Indexer: Lisa Scholey

Printed in Poland by L&C Printing Group

The paper used in this book comes from the wood pulp of sustainably managed forests.

A NOTE FROM THE PUBLISHER
We want to try to offset the environmental impacts of carbon during the production of our books and journals. This year we will plant 45 trees with Easy Treesie. The Easy Treesie—Crann Project organises children to plant trees. Crann—'Trees for Ireland' is a membership-based, non-profit, registered charity (CHY13698) uniting people with a love of trees.

Royal Irish Academy is a member of Publishing Ireland, the Irish book publishers' association

This publication has been supported by

Grangegorman
Development Agency
Gníomhaireacht Forbartha
Ghráinseach Ghormáin

GRANGEGORMAN
HISTORIES

5 4 3 2 1

This book is dedicated to Regina, Eoin and Isabel.

# CONTENTS

## A note from the author

Throughout this book, I have used original language and terminology from the past and from various archives and reports, except where explicitly indicated otherwise. This reflects an attempt to optimise fidelity to historical sources and does not indicate a broader endorsement of such terminology in contemporary settings. I anonymised individual case histories to maintain confidentiality. It is hoped that, in the future, the regulatory framework surrounding access, confidentiality, and disclosure of historical records will be revised to allow historians and other researchers to give clearer voice to those who were admitted to our institutions in the past. They deserve to be heard and seen.

# "I will not say I am sorry you are dying"

**Mary G. was admitted to Grangegorman District Asylum in Dublin**, Ireland's largest mental institution, in early 1908. A 28-year old married woman with a baby of three months, Mary had refused food for the previous six days. Archival case-notes from the asylum record that Mary was paranoid. She 'heard tapping at night. People followed her in the street...They said everything they could say'. At night, she heard the voices of 'people who are dead'. When asked her name, Mary responded: 'Queen Victoria'.

One week after admission to the cavernous institution, Mary did not know where she was: 'Says she is in the ambulance'. Two weeks after admission, Mary could not remember her doctor's name and reported hearing 'voices going about. Does not know what they say. Restless'.

Over a year later, Mary was still in the asylum and was described by the doctor as 'very dull. Does not know who I am or where she is'. Nonetheless, Mary did 'a little work' on the ward, probably needlework or laundry. The following January, after two years in the asylum, Mary's six-month review by the doctor was even more terse: 'Dull, stupid. Will not answer a single question. Works.' In July, the doctor 'couldn't get a word out of her, only a foolish smile'.

Three months later, the clinical notes recorded that Mary was 'dying of phthisis' (tuberculosis, which was common in the large, unhygienic asylums). Later that month, Mary's sister wrote to her from England:

My Dear Sister,

I hear from the doctor that you cannot live long. I am not surprised as it was the opinion I formed of you when I saw you last August. Now, what I want to know is, is there anything you would like that you can't get in hospital, I mean in the way of fruit or cakes? If you will let me know I will send you some money. I am sure any of the nurses would get anything.

I will not say I am sorry you are dying. The wonder to me is you have lived so long, considering what you must have suffered the last 10 years in poverty in Dublin. Hoping you will have a happy death, if you are not already reaping the reward of all your sufferings here,

Your affectionate sister,

Jane.

In Mary's medical file, the doctor recorded that Mary's 'sister sent her the appended letter which I did not give her'. At the time, it was common for doctors to withhold letters that might upset patients, even at the end of life.

Like so many others, Mary died in the asylum, just a day or two after her sister's letter arrived, having spent the last three years of her life in Grangegorman. Apart from the presence of the asylum staff, Mary died alone, abandoned by her family, her community and a society that offered only cold institutional comforts to the destitute mentally ill.

How did people like Mary end up in this hopeless, tragic situation? And why? And what were the final years of Mary's life like, behind asylum walls?

These are the questions that inspired this book.

"Very deleterious morally, physically,& mentally."

# 'It is a mistake to suppose that the insane are very different from the sane.'

Dr Conolly Norman, Resident Medical Superintendent (RMS)
Richmond District Asylum, Grangegorman (1905)[1]

The mental asylums are Ireland's awkward institutions. They were designed to treat and contain the mentally ill but soon assumed a life of their own: meeting the complex needs of troubled families (often unrelated to mental illness); alleviating social problems in surrounding communities (especially during times of poverty, famine or political unrest); and—possibly most of all—supporting local economies by employing tens of thousands of people, often in areas of the country with limited alternative employment.

Ireland's enormous asylums were secular institutions, run by government, so it is not possible to place responsibility for them with the Roman Catholic Church, which is commonly associated with many of the other excesses of Ireland's institutional past. The church never became deeply involved in the asylums, its attention occupied, perhaps, by its extensive involvement in general hospitals, maternity care, schools, orphanages and laundries. Or perhaps the mentally ill were seen as undeserving? In any case, the story of the Irish asylums is more complex and troubling than any simple explanation permits, and does not lend itself to easy exposition.

Even the language we use to discuss the asylums is contested and uneasy. Acceptable terminology moved from 'lunatic asylums' to 'district asylums' to 'mental hospitals' to 'psychiatric institutions' and, finally, to 'inpatient mental health units'. People suffered from 'madness', then 'lunacy', then 'psychiatric illness' and now 'mental disorder'. And there were, at all times, a range of other, less acceptable and frankly offensive terms. In all respects, the story of Ireland's asylum system is an awkward, complex, contested and unresolved one.

But it is also a story about well-intentioned efforts to care for the mentally ill, house the destitute, accommodate the intellectually disabled and provide some kind of 'asylum' to people whom Irish society was only too ready to label as odd, different, 'other'.

As a result of these competing complexities, the history of the Irish asylums can be explored in many different ways: by examining the process of negotiation that resulted in so many admissions occurring in the first place,[2] by telling the stories of any of the numerous hospitals that were required as a result,[3] or by presenting the alarming statistics of the asylum system as a whole, as Ireland built and filled more asylum beds per head of population than any other country in the world.[4]

These are the stories that fill this book, to varying degrees. But this is primarily a book about *people,* telling its story through case histories drawn from the archives of one institution, the Richmond District Asylum in Grangegorman, Dublin, the establishment that lay at the very heart of Ireland's network of institutions for the mentally ill and provided the example for others to emulate.[5] The Richmond was where new treatments were introduced, new ideas developed, and more patients treated than at any other asylum in the country. For better or for worse, the Richmond, also known as 'Grangegorman' and, later, 'St Brendan's Hospital', set the tone for Ireland's mass institutionalisation of the mentally ill throughout the 1800s and much of the 1900s.

The stories are both extraordinary and disturbing. In the late 1850s, for example, four decades after the asylum opened, Máire A., a 23-year old single 'servant' was admitted to the Richmond. Máire was transferred from the neighbouring Richmond Penitentiary (prison) and diagnosed with 'melancholia', cause 'unknown'. On admission to the Richmond, Máire's 'reaction to questions' was 'fairly prompt and coherent'. She was 'not devoid of intelligence' but had 'a slight tendency to hypochondriasis'.

The medical notes record the stark circumstances under which Máire was declared a 'dangerous lunatic' and committed to the asylum:

> She describes clearly the incident of her brother asking her to come for a walk with him and then taking her to the police office. Her hair was shaved off and she was detained in the jail. After some years she was transferred here. She says that previous to her arrest, something very terrible was in her and wouldn't let her rest in the bed and made her break a window. She speaks as if of some force possessing her, though she denies that it was the devil.

In the asylum, Máire was 'an industrious working patient for many years'. She was 'very tidy and respectable in appearance', with 'mild chronic melancholia'.

But despite the 'mildness' of Máire's diagnosis, despite her good conduct, and despite her industriousness in the institution, she was to spend the rest of her life in the cramped, crowded wards of the Richmond: devoid of personal possessions, utterly deprived of privacy, with straw for bedding, and with no control over her daily routine. Máire took her

meals in vast, noisy dining halls, washed in communal bathrooms, and slept on wards that were crowded, disturbed and often dangerous. With wearying inevitability, Máire eventually died in the institution, succumbing to 'heart disease' at the age of 68, some 45 years after she was first admitted.

Máire's story was not an unusual one in Ireland or elsewhere during the nineteenth century.[6] But while many countries established asylums for the mentally ill during this period, Ireland's rate of admission rose faster than those in other countries, was higher at its peak, and was slower to decline.[7] How did this happen?

In 1817 Robert Peel (1788–1850), Chief Secretary, set up a select committee to examine provision for 'the lunatic poor in Ireland'. The Right Honourable Denis Browne (a Mayo member of parliament) described the plight of the mentally ill in rural Ireland prior to the asylums:

> There is nothing so shocking as madness in the cabin of the peasant, where the man is out labouring in the fields for his bread, and the care of the woman of the house is scarcely sufficient for the attendance on the children. When a strong young man or woman gets the complaint [madness], the only way they have to manage is by making a hole in the floor of the cabin not high enough for the person to stand up in, with a crib over it to prevent his getting up; the hole is about five feet deep, and they give the wretched being his food there, and there he generally dies.[8]

Prior to the creation of asylums such as the Richmond, the mentally ill in Ireland were either mistreated and restrained in family homes, consigned to lives of vagrancy and early death, or confined in houses of industry (workhouses) or prisons, often for years.[9] The first dedicated asylum that sought to address this problem in Ireland was St Patrick's Hospital in Dublin, founded in 1746 following the benevolent bequest of author Jonathan Swift (1667–1745).[10] In his wickedly satirical 'Verses on the death of Dr Swift', the great thinker, churchman and author of *Gulliver's travels* anticipated his own death and legacy:

> He gave the little Wealth he had,
> To build a House for Fools and Mad:
> And shew'd by one satyric Touch,
> No Nation wanted it so much.

St Patrick's was, however, a private, charitable establishment that did not have the broader, population-level responsibilities of government-run institutions. Greater, systematic provision was clearly needed, especially for the 'lunatic poor'.

One particularly enterprising doctor, William Saunders Hallaran, founded a public asylum in Cork in 1792 to accommodate 24 patients, and a private asylum in 1799. By 1822, Cork Lunatic Asylum had expanded to cater for over 300 patients. In 1810, Hallaran, alarmed by the relentless demand for asylum beds, published Ireland's first textbook of psychiatry, the splendidly titled *Enquiry into the Causes producing the Extraordinary Addition to the Number of Insane together with Extended Observations on the Cure of Insanity with Hints as to the Better Management of Public Asylums for Insane Persons.*[11] A second edition of Hallaran's insightful, witty, shocking and slightly hysterical book appeared in 1818.[12]

Hallaran was most concerned about the apparent increase of insanity in Ireland and the ever-increasing number of people presenting to asylums in search of admission. He related this 'extraordinary increase of insanity in Ireland' to both 'corporeal [i.e. bodily] excitement' and 'mental excitement', which he linked with social unrest, 'terror from religious enthusiasm' and 'the unrestrained use and abuse of ardent spirits'. Alcohol was especially pernicious. Once a person had developed 'the habit of daily intoxication', Halloran wrote, 'the countenance now bespeaks a dreary waste of mind and body; all is confusion and wild extravagance'. In Hallaran's view, the solution lay in reforming revenue laws, limiting availability of alcohol, and increasing the *quality* of alcohol consumed.[13]

But most of all, as Hallaran pointed out, greater provision was needed to accommodate and treat the destitute mentally ill. In 1806, the Hospitals and Infirmaries (Ireland) Act enabled Grand Juries to present money for wards for lunatics in connection with County Infirmaries and for the maintenance of asylums in connection with the Houses of Industry—charitable institutions that offered relief and accommodation to the destitute. These workhouses were funded through taxation, including a house tax. There was, however, enormous pressure on the Dublin House of Industry in particular, so in 1810 government finances were made available to build a public asylum to be named the Richmond Asylum, in honour of the Duke of Richmond, Lord Lieutenant of Ireland.

Dr Alexander Jackson (1767–1848), a physician at the Dublin House of Industry, had a keen interest in the mentally ill and provided advice on the new asylum, which was to be located at Grangegorman, just north of the River Liffey in Dublin. The architect was Francis Johnston, whose other work included Dublin's General Post Office. The plan for the new asylum at Grangegorman was similar to that of Bethlem Asylum in England. The first patients from the House of Industry were transferred there in 1814 and the Richmond officially opened the following year, as legislation established its governors as a corporation with perpetual succession.

There were fifteen governors: William Harvey MD, the physician general; George Renny MD, the surgeon general; Philip Crampton MD, the director general of hospitals; Robert Percival MD; Judge Arthur Moore; Reverend Willian O'Connor; Reverend James Horner; John David La Touche; Peter La Touche, Junior; William Disney; John Leslie Foster; William Harding; James Henthorn; Edward Houghton; and Francis L'Estrange. All of these men had various involvements in charitable provision in the past: John David La Touche, William Disney and George Renny had been asked by the Lord Lieutenant to report on the management of various charities in 1808, while James Henthorn, Edward Houghton, Francis L'Estrange and the two clergymen had been the governors of the House of Industry, where Henthorn had also been surgeon for 33 years following its opening in 1773.[14]

Over the following two centuries, the Richmond Asylum expanded rapidly, admitted tens of thousands of patients from all corners of Ireland and changed its name several times, to the Richmond District Lunatic Asylum in 1830, Grangegorman Mental Hospital in 1925, and St Brendan's Hospital in 1958. 'Grangegorman', as it was often known, continuously pioneered new treatments for mental illness in Ireland, ranging from 'moral management' in the nineteenth century (Chapter 2) to the biological treatments of the twentieth century (Chapter 9), and it served as a model for the vast network of district asylums that was established across the country throughout the remainder of the nineteenth century.

There were three identifiable waves of asylum-building in Ireland. The first wave brought four further district asylums during the 1820s and five more by 1835. Legislation in 1845 then made provision for the Central Criminal Lunatic Asylum in Dundrum, Dublin and the large Eglinton Asylum in Cork, which opened in the early 1850s.

More asylums were later opened, in Mullingar (1855), Letterkenny (1866) and Castlcbar (1866), the latter two designed by George Wilkinson, better known for designing workhouses. There was endless controversy about the asylum-building process during the 1850s, resulting in a scathing report by London architect T.L Donaldson and James Wilkes, medical officer at Stafford Lunatic Asylum, supporting local concerns about how building work was being directed from Dublin.[15]

In 1855, a clearly frustrated Select Committee of the House of Commons interrogated Dr John Nugent, Inspector-General of Lunatic Asylums in Ireland, at some length, to try to figure out who was responsible for monitoring the building of so many asylums, a rather opaque process that was rapidly slipping out of anyone's control. As reported in the Select Committee meeting minutes:

> *During the building of the asylum, is it any part of your duty or practice to visit the asylum?*
> Nugent: It is not part of our duty to do that, because we have no authority one way or another. I invariably go and look at the asylum as they go on building, but I have no authority whatever to interfere; I may suggest, and that is all.
>
> *During the building of the asylum, is it the fact that you make a great many visits to that asylum?*
> Yes.
>
> *And that you make different suggestions and remarks upon its condition to the Board of Works?*
> Yes, I do.

*Have you done so in all cases?*
In various cases I have done so.

*So that not only when the asylum is complete, and handed over to the Board of Governors, do you see it, but also when the building is going on you are practically aware of its condition?*
Yes, I may go and look at it, but I have no authority to interfere. It occasionally has happened that I have given suggestions, some of which have been adopted, others have not; therefore I am not answerable or responsible for anything connected with the building; that rests with the Board of Works. I may suggest, but I have no authority whatever to direct.[16]

Nugent's responses simply added to the Select Committee's confusion because Nugent appeared to inspect the building works as the asylums were erected but did not have clear responsibility to do so. As a result, the Board of Works was entirely free to ignore his advice, as it frequently did, resulting in a network of asylums of uncertain provenance, uneven quality and decidedly unsatisfactory standards.

The Committee was none the wiser at the end of its enquiry. The only thing entirely clear was that asylums were now unstoppable. The third phase of asylum-building raced ahead and included an asylum in Ennis (with a fine Florentine palazzo) (1868), the Monaghan asylum (the first with a villa or pavilion format) (1869) and the auxiliary asylum to the Richmond, in Portrane, County Dublin (later known as St Ita's). An asylum was also built in Antrim (1899) so that, by 1900, around 21,000 people, or 0.5 per cent of the entire population of the 32 counties of Ireland, were accommodated in district asylums, with a small number of the mentally ill still in workhouses.[17] The era of the asylum had well and truly arrived—led by the Richmond at Grangegorman.

Even with this provision of thousands of new asylum beds, however, demand greatly exceeded supply. There were growing problems in the new institutions, which were clearly too large, grossly unhygienic and—perhaps most disturbingly—filled with people who did not need to be there. In 1906, Dr Conolly Norman (1853–1908), progressive Resident Medical Superintendent (RMS) at the Richmond, bemoaned (in the language of the times) the number of people with intellectual disability inappropriately placed in the new institutions:

> The whole class of idiots as they appear in our public asylums are very lamentable, very pitiable, and usually in this country it indicates shameful neglect, because almost all idiots are capable, if taken early, of being improved...In this country they don't get that early care and attention...In this country they drift into workhouses and are treated with organised neglect. This is very deleterious morally, physically, and mentally, and every other way.[18]

The unseemly and apparently indefensible rush to institutionalise the mentally ill and intellectually disabled needs to be understood in the context of nineteenth-century Ireland. If a person was mentally ill or intellectually disabled, families often felt they had few options other than to seek committal to an asylum. Ireland did not have many private asylums during this period, and providing care at home was the preserve of the wealthy. As a result, Irish communities used asylums in complex and often quite subtle ways, to meet the needs of families and the broader community. This regrettable state of affairs was made possible by a set of legal arrangements that made committal to asylums excessively easy and discharge excessively difficult—as demonstrated by the case of Máire A., who spent 45 years of her life in the Richmond for no good reason.

This book explores why people like Máire A. were constrained to live so much of their lives behind asylum walls, and what asylum life was like for them.

The book examines the process of admission to the Richmond (Chapter 1), the 'moral management' approach to care in the nineteenth century (Chapter 2), daily life inside the asylum (Chapter 3), the central role of food in the Richmond (Chapter 4), physical illnesses, such as tuberculosis (Chapter 5), the lives of asylum staff (Chapter 6), the Richmond War Hospital and its treatment of 'shell shock' owing to the First World War (Chapter 7), the Richmond during Ireland's revolutionary years (Chapter 8), new treatments for mental illness in the early twentieth century (Chapter 9), and more recent history (Chapter 10).

Most of all, this book tries to make sense of the story of Máire A. and the many others like her who found themselves caught up in Ireland's extraordinary and sometimes shameful asylum system. These are the stories of people who were, for various reasons, consigned to institutions, often for several decades if not for life, with doctors unable to discharge them home and families either unable or unwilling to take them back.

How did it come to this? What kind of lives did these people lead inside the asylums? What became of them? And, most importantly, what can we learn from astonishing institutions like the Richmond, which helped some people, betrayed others, and ultimately spun out of control, in full view of the professions, the public, the media, and politicians of the day? What, if anything, have we learned from Grangegorman?

Reading over the archives and official reports, three themes become clear. First, the intentions of those who founded, funded, and ran the asylums were fundamentally altruistic. Seized by the plight of the 'lunatic poor', Irish society – like societies elsewhere – built institutions designed to care and cure. The intentions were excellent, even if the resultant mental hospitals were substantially less so.

Second, in an institution like a large mental hospital, emphasis inevitably shifts from providing individual care to managing the institution. The societal hunger for simple solutions to complex problems leads to the use of institutions to meet complicated social needs which often have little to do with the original purpose of the establishment. In other words, institutions expand inexorably, deteriorate inevitably, and are ultimately dysfunctional. The mental hospitals are a perfect example, as this book will hopefully demonstrate.

Third, the 'lessons' to be learned from the history of the Richmond Asylum are not simple, if lessons can be learned at all. Like all of Ireland's asylums, Grangegorman was an extraordinary creation. It reflected much that was good and a great deal that was dark in Irish society. Its history should be told, absorbed, and understood, insofar as this is possible. It is a history that cannot be reduced to simple lessons, but neither can it be ignored. That is why there are case histories from the Grangegorman archive throughout this book, to add human stories to the statistics and historical facts discussed, to remember the lives spent behind asylum walls, to give voice to the forgotten.

# "I might as well be what I am"

'The great question which constantly arises in mental disease is whether the patient should be sent to an asylum, which—no matter how we gild the pill—means sending him to imprisonment, sometimes life-long imprisonment.'

Dr Conolly Norman, RMS, Richmond District Asylum (1905)[1]

Máire A. was admitted to Grangegorman under the Criminal Lunatics (Ireland) Act, 1838 or, to use its full title, 'An Act to make more Effectual Provision for the Prevention of Offences by Insane Persons in Ireland'. This notorious legislation was passed following the murder of Nathaniel Sneyd, a prominent wine merchant with the House of Sneyd, French and Barton, by a person with apparent mental illness, in Dublin on Monday, 29 July 1833.[2] Five days later, the *Manchester Guardian* reported on the 'horrid assassination':

> Mr Nathaniel Sneyd, a respectable and extensive wine merchant of this city, has just been shot by a man named Mason, who came up to him in Westmoreland Street, at the corner of

the Bank of Ireland, and deliberately shot him through the head. The man was apprehended on the spot, and brought into the police office...Mr Sneyd died on Wednesday morning. An inquest was held on the body, and returned a verdict of wilful murder against Mason. It seems probable that he was insane at the time he committed the murder.[3]

Given the drama of this event, legislation was soon developed with the primary purpose of containing the insane. There was no parliamentary debate about the resultant Act, the chief purpose of which was to protect the public from the dangers supposedly posed by the mentally ill.[4] The legislation's terms of confinement were extremely vague and permitted committal to county prisons or bridewells and then transfer to asylums, although there were commonly delays of months or even years before the move to an asylum (as in the case of Máire A).

During the committal process, medical evidence could be heard but was not mandatory, and certificates were signed by two magistrates (rather than doctors). This simple, unjust mechanism soon became the admission pathway of choice for families seeking asylum care for relatives. A habit grew of encouraging a mentally ill or intellectually disabled person to commit or threaten to commit a minor offence in order to facilitate committal under the 1838 Act.[5] Discharge was only possible when the patient's sanity was medically certified to the lord lieutenant by the asylum doctors.

Once the 1838 Act was passed, transfers from prisons to asylums commenced with great haste: thirteen people were referred from gaol to the Richmond alone in the first half of July 1838.[6] The asylum was already full but the chief secretary, Lord Morpeth (George Howard, 7th Earl of Carlisle), stated that these transfers were to be accepted anyway, regardless of the number of patients already in the asylum. Overcrowding was, therefore, rapid, inevitable and unstoppable.

The horrified asylum doctors objected loudly, pointing out that many of the transfers from prisons were utterly inappropriate, but the transfers kept on coming and inpatient numbers kept on rising, especially since discharge was far from simple. Objections in the House of Commons and an 1843 amendment requiring at least one credible witness in each case made little difference. The 1838 Act quickly established itself the main mechanism for warehousing thousands of people in the Irish asylums. In the 1850s, committals of 'dangerous lunatics' accounted for 42 per cent of male and 32 per cent of female admissions to district lunatic asylums, and by the early 1890s, these proportions had risen to 76 per cent for men and 67 per cent for women, with some regional variation.[7]

One of the most vocal critics of the new legislation was the newly appointed 'physician extraordinary' at the Richmond, Dr John Mollan. Mollan was a native of Newry who received his education in Edinburgh and was appointed to the Richmond in January 1836. He had considerable medical experience across various Dublin hospitals and a particular interest in the insane.[8] Two years after his appointment, the energetic Mollan presented a detailed 'statistical report of the Richmond Lunatic Asylum' at the Evening Meeting of the College of Physicians, on 26 March 1838.[9]

Mollan reported that there were 608 admissions to the Richmond over the five-year period between January 1833 and December 1837. The most common cause of insanity among women was 'fright' and among men was 'intemperance and abuse of ardent spirits'; i.e. alcohol, as William Saunders Hallaran had warned. Other causes included 'pecuniary losses and reverses of fortune', 'domestic disagreements and bad treatment by relatives', 'jealousy', 'religion', 'pride' and 'close confinement and study'. 'Seduction', 'change of life consequent on marriage', 'love and disappointed affections' were more common among women than men, and there was a single case of 'excessive fondness for music' (male).

Physical causes of insanity included injuries, fever, cholera, influenza, scarlatina (scarlet fever, an infection), erysipelas (an infection with skin rash) and 'abuse of mercury'. Mercury was used to treat virtually every disease in the 1800s, but it could also be poisonous. Mollan recounted one case in some detail:

> A farmer about twenty-seven years of age was admitted into the asylum, after having been nearly four years in a state of dementia [a catch-all term for any mental illness], in consequence, it was reported, of the improper use of mercury. He was listless and taciturn, and would only reply to questions about himself, by telling his name and place of abode; his general health was unimpaired, and his appetite was good, but before commencing his meals he always required the assurance of some of the attendants that the food was good, and proper for him to eat.

At first, he refused to engage in any occupation, but being otherwise amenable, and shewing no vicious propensity, a wheel-barrow was placed before him, and a man at either side took him each by a hand, and fixing them on the handles of the barrow, he was gently urged to the use of it; finding this plan persevered in, he soon consented to work by himself; and afterwards taking to the use of the spade he proved himself an excellent workman. In a short time an improvement was apparent in his mental state, he became gradually more intelligent and communicative; his recovery proceeded without interruption, and he was discharged quite well after a residence of eleven months in the asylum.

Mollan made no mention of treatment in this case, other than giving the man a wheel-barrow, but reported that the outcome was good. This benign sounding case, however, belied the harsh truth revealed in Mollan's statistics: the rate of admission at the Richmond was increasing rapidly, and by 1838 the institution was overcrowded and under pressure to admit yet more people:

The house was planned originally for the reception of 236 patients, but by alterations subsequently made, 288 can now be admitted; and yet, owing to the accumulation of incurable cases during a series of years, the accommodation is found to be inadequate to meet the wants of the district, and the asylum labours under the disadvantage of not being at all times able to receive patients immediately on their being attacked [by mental illness], a circumstance which has an important effect on the result of treatment.

When the Richmond could not 'receive patients immediately', they were left to languish in prisons while they awaited transfer to the asylum. Many, like Máire A., waited for years. Interestingly, Mollan reported that the majority of the asylum's patients were from the middle and upper classes:

> The class of labourers, the lowest in the social scale, though numerically greater than all the others, does not furnish a fourth of these cases. As we ascend in society, mental cultivation is greater, more means of vicious indulgence exist, and greater liability to the vicissitudes of fortune; and we also find a greater proportional number of cases of insanity; not, indeed, in a regularly progressive ratio, but speaking generally, in the middle and upper classes of society, insanity is more common than in the lowest.

In fact, it is likely that far greater numbers of 'labourers' languished in workhouses and prisons for longer periods than those 'in the middle and upper classes of society', who ended up in the Richmond, which was seen as preferable to either a prison or a workhouse. By 1838, there were 284 patients in the Richmond, and 1,610 throughout

Ireland's entire system of district asylums. Of these, 881 were 'incurable' and 136 were 'idiotic' (i.e. possibly had an intellectual disability). Outside of the public district asylums, there were 148 people with apparent mental illness or intellectual disability in St Patrick's Hospital, 1,008 in workhouses, and 363 in various other locations such as infirmaries, gaols and private asylums, which comprised a small but significant element within Ireland's by-now flourishing asylum system.[10]

Religious themes featured strongly in many patients' symptoms and concerns, and patients usually attended church in the asylum. Medical notes record that Máire A. 'used to fret about her soul and thought she had none. When told that her soul is safe...she replies 'It wouldn't be safe in the life I am having in this place.' She thinks she lives a bad life. [She] does not go to church...Seems to admit that she ought to go to church. Says she was asked to go recently by her attendant. Pressed on the subject of going to church, says she thought they were not kind. "I might as well be what I am".'

Given the rapidly increasing asylum population at the Richmond and elsewhere, and the clear injustice of the 1838 Act, the chief secretary of Ireland Lord Naas attempted to enact reforms with the Lunacy Law Amendment Bill 1859. But it was not until 1867 that the 1838 legislation was finally amended, with the effect of ending confinement in gaols prior to entering asylums and requiring magistrates to call a dispensary medical officer to examine the patient and sign the certificate.[11] This reform, although positive in its way, made little difference to the increasing numbers: in 1893, the Inspectors of Lunatics reported a small fall in the number of certified 'idiots' or people with intellectual disability (from 7,033 in 1861 to 6,243 in 1891), but (yet again) a dramatic rise in the number of 'lunatics' or people with mental illness (from 7,065 in 1861 to 14,945 in 1891).[12] Clearly, the asylums could not be stopped.

Clinical cases from the Richmond archives demonstrate the wide variety of reasons for admission which pushed these numbers up as the nineteenth century progressed. In 1869, Bernard S., a 'labourer', was committed to the Richmond as a 'dangerous lunatic'. A farmer's son, Bernard had set fire to his father's home, assaulted his step-mother and stabbed a man in the legs with a pitchfork. Several months earlier, on a boat from England, Bernard had been reportedly overwhelmed by fear during a severe gale and had been intermittently unwell since then. A medical certificate supported Bernard's committal to the Richmond, where he stayed for the remaining thirteen years of his life, until he died of pneumonia in 1882. At the time of his death, a letter from Bernard's family indicated that Bernard's 'father is dead fifteen months and his mother is dead and his brothers are in America'. The family had 'no means to bury him', so Bernard, utterly abandoned by everyone, was buried by the asylum.

While Bernard showed no signs of mental illness at any point, the records of other patients show at least some evidence of psychiatric symptoms. Patrick R., a 21-year old single man, was committed to the Richmond in the early 1880s for 'saying he would drown himself' and 'attempting to set fire to the house' where he lived with his mother and sister. Patrick was diagnosed with 'mania' but was also 'very low' at times. In 1898, seventeen years after admission, Patrick was still in the Richmond and was 'a quiet and useful man about the ward when at his best',

although at times he developed a 'vacant, scared look' and whispered inaudibly to himself, seemingly 'in response to voices'.

Patrick was seen by Dr Daniel Frederick Rambaut (1865– 1937), a colourful medical figure who spent nine years as assistant medical officer and pathologist in the Richmond.[13] Rambaut wrote an extraordinarily perceptive note in Patrick's medical file, in which he described a clinical pattern that would later be known as 'cycloid psychosis':

> Patient has a period of about nine weeks which is repeated with great regularity.
>
> 1st week, during which he gradually passes from his sane state to a state of much restlessness, agitation and incoherence. The first thing that is noticed is that he won't get up in the morning and make his bed. He becomes gradually more restless and incoherent, untidy and filthy in his habits.
>
> 2nd week, gradually becoming worse.
>
> 3rd week, in which he reaches his worst state. He is now restless, agitated, chattering and whispering incoherently...He now passes urine and faeces in his clothes, licks up sputum and all manner of filth from the floor, stuffs his mouth with food, and almost chokes when attempting to swallow it. He runs about shutting the windows if they are open and opening them if they are shut.
>
> 4th week, the above are less marked.
>
> 5th week, gradually becomes more tidy and clean, and less restless and incoherent, and begins to work and make his bed.

6th, 7th, 8th and 9th weeks, during which
he works well, is clean, a quiet eater and can
be trusted. Talks coherently.'

Patrick continued in this episodically disturbed state
for many years and was eventually transferred from the
Richmond to its sister asylum in Portrane, where he died
in 1912, after 31 years in the asylums.

In addition to such prolonged stays in the asylums
themselves, there was also a great deal of 'trans-instu-
tionalisation', as people were moved between prisons,
workhouses, general hospitals and mental asylums,
transferring from one institution to another, often multiple times and sometimes for no discernible reason. On
31 January 1907 the chairman of the Richmond District
Asylum Joint Committee highlighted the inappropriate-
ness of many such transfers to the Richmond:

A large number of our admissions come here
direct from workhouses. I have looked up the
exact numbers and find they average about 30
per cent of total admissions. During the last
four financial years 709 patients came from
workhouses. I do not think I would be very
much in error in estimating that 50 per cent of
these 709 admissions would come under the
head of Chronic and Harmless Lunatics, and
probably at the present time there are not far
short of 700 or 800 cases in the whole institution who could be so classified. The 76th
section of the Local Government Act of 1898
provides for the establishment of auxiliary
asylums for such cases.[14]

Despite the Committee's concerns, however, the Richmond was by now an embedded part of an intense geographical cluster of institutions that emerged in the 1800s and included a prison, a workhouse and a series of hospitals between which people were transferred frequently, pointlessly and often inappropriately.[15] Eileen M. is a good example of a person whose transfer from a workhouse to the Richmond was at best inappropriate and at worst fatal.

Eileen was admitted to the Richmond from a workhouse in 1905. The workhouse master declared that Eileen had been of 'unsound mind' for 'about six months' and was 'destitute, having no funds out of which her maintenance in the asylum can be met wholly or in part, and having no friends who are able or willing to support her in a private or other asylum for insane'. He also made the rather remarkable claim that Eileen had been a resident of County Wicklow for some 110 years prior to arriving in the workhouse and was now aged 113 years. She was married with six children.

The chief reason for Eileen's transfer to the Richmond was that she assaulted the maid in the workhouse and was unmanageably restless there, 'continually looking for her son. Climbs over bed looking for Mick'. Eileen 'violently' resisted 'being put back to bed' and used 'filthy language'. Her admission to the Richmond was supported by a medical certificate, a recommendation by a Justice of the Peace and an undertaking from the workhouse master to remove Eileen back to the workhouse if the asylum requested that he do so.

At the time of her admission to the Richmond, Eileen's son Michael stated that he believed her to be 112 years of age, and that he was her youngest child, now 'about 67 years old'. Eileen had always been 'hale and hearty', he said. Eileen herself claimed to be blind and 'slightly deaf' but was neither. She also claimed to have been 11 years of age at the time of the 1798 rebellion, which would have made her an even more remarkable 118 years of age when she arrived at the Richmond in 1905. Later, asked again about her age, she answered: 'Bedad, it's past counting'.

Five days after her admission to the Richmond, one of Eileen's friends wrote to the doctors, expressing outrage:

> Dear Sir, I am more than surprised such steps should be taken with this poor old woman whom I have known for many years. To send her to an asylum as mad is simply ridiculous, especially one of her age, and the official who took this on their shoulders should be placed in her position.

In the asylum, Eileen was 'restless', 'very feeble' and suffered from bronchitis. She thought she was still in the workhouse and did not know the date. She was incontinent, 'noisy, restless and troublesome', and continually 'trying to get out of bed to get "Mick's dinner"'.

By the end of January 1907, after almost a year and a half in the Richmond, Eileen 'got dysentery [inflammation of the intestine] and is very bad—dying'. Staff also discovered that she had a broken rib despite no recent 'history of accident or violence'. The doctor attributed the rib fracture to Eileen's generally debilitated state: 'She is so very old and helpless that in my opinion the mere fact of moving her in the bed to change her would be enough to break a rib as she is <u>very</u> heavy indeed'.

Eileen died in 1907, two years after admission to the Richmond. The following month, the asylum sought to definitively establish her age and discovered that the 1851 census recorded just one person of her name with six children in her parish—but her age was given as 40 years in 1851. That would have made her 96 at the time of her death—old enough to have heard talk of the 1798 rebellion, but not old enough to have witnessed it.

Either way, the final years of Eileen's long life were spent in a debilitated and likely demented state in a work-house and, later, asylum, bringing a distressing end to a complex, troubled life. Most tragically, there is no evidence in the Richmond records that Eileen suffered from any mental illness, apart from confusion in later life, which was probably caused or worsened by the institutional settings in which she spent her final years.

Other women demonstrated similarly complex mixes of difficult social circumstances and psychiatric symptoms that were probably more attributable to their life situations than to mental illness. Teresa H., a 23-year old married woman, was admitted to the Richmond from another workhouse in 1906, with the belief that 'chloroform was administered to her'. Teresa had five children, the youngest just ten months old, and this was her first admission. She complained of a sore back, stating that a nurse in the workhouse had kicked her. Admission notes described Teresa as 'a voluble little woman who looks only about 18 or 20 though she has had five children in five years':

> Says she and her husband fought and proceeds
> to tell a long, tangled tale of family squabbles
> but the principal point is that she believes that

chloroform was given to her [in the work-
house] through 'cracks in the ceiling', and
then proceeds to show me her <u>hair</u> which she
says has chloroform on it.

The day after her admission to the Richmond, Teresa
was 'most restless, troublesome, trying to get away':

Says her husband was prosecuted for ill-treat-
ing the children and herself. He drank and
beat her. Her mother was killed a little over
a year ago. She fell from a train. Patient used
to see something white coming and heard her
mother's voice bidding her leave the house.
Asked was this reality or fancy, [she] says it
really happened.

Two weeks after admission, Teresa was 'much quieter
than she was', but persisted with the belief that she was
poisoned and would 'not do <u>any</u> work' in the asylum,
unlike other female patients who were commonly engaged
in cooking, cleaning or needle-work. Teresa was 'very
stubborn'. Eventually, Teresa started 'working well' in
the laundry, although she still believed 'that her mother's
ghost appeared to her and talked to her'.

After eight months in the asylum, Teresa was ready for
discharge, but the doctor reported procedural problems:

[The other doctor] passed her for discharge
last month to care of sister, who refuses to
take her. She will not go back to her husband
if she can help it, as he beat her, she says. I am

bringing her up again tomorrow [to the Board, for approval for discharge] to see what can be done. She is quiet and steady but still believes [that chloroform] was put on her—but I do not think it would influence her conduct in any way, if at large.

Teresa was eventually discharged, 'recovered', in early 1907, after ten months in the Richmond.

Some admissions were even shorter. In 1907, Michael B, a twenty-year old single man, was admitted from the nearby North Dublin Union workhouse:

Patient has been born and bred in the Union. He was in his right mind till four days ago when he became restless and threatened the Master [of the Union]'s life. He has refused food since, save for milk. Patient seems quiet. He is weak-minded. He imagines he has been injured by the Master of the Union...His general health is fair...His left eye is glass.

Over the following weeks, Michael, who likely had an intellectual disability rather than mental illness, worked in the asylum grounds and on the asylum farm. He reported hearing noises, 'like a piano playing', but was generally 'quiet and well-behaved'. He was discharged, 'recovered', after five weeks in the Richmond. Having spent all his early life in the workhouse, followed by a spell in the Richmond, it is likely Michael lived the rest of his days back in the workhouse or in some other institution, and ultimately died in one.

Many other patients who were admitted to the Richmond spent the remainders of their lives there or in Portrane, often owing to single instances of attempted suicide or quite vague threats against other people. In early 1881, Francis P., a 26-year old single man, was committed to the Richmond as a 'dangerous lunatic' having 'threatened to take the life' of his brother. Clinical notes record that Francis was 'suicidal at times' and 'violent and incoherent in his manner'. He had 'shot himself about 18 months ago through the upper portion of left lung, ball entering below the 3rd rib and coming out in the supras-capular fossa [above the shoulder blade at the back of the upper chest]. He does not remember doing it but remembers being under treatment for the surgery'. Francis spent ten years in the Richmond before being transferred to Portrane, where he died many years later.

As a result of these and many other similar cases, the numbers in asylums, later called 'mental hospitals', continued to rise alarmingly during the first half of the twentieth century. The Mental Treatment Act of 1945 sought to address this problem by introducing new admission procedures to replace the disastrous provisions of the 1838 Act. The 1945 legislation heralded a new emphasis on voluntary admission and introduced a range of other measures designed to improve practices and standards of care. But admission rates continued to climb inexorably until the late 1950s, at which point Ireland had the highest rate of psychiatric bed availability internationally.[16]

Over this time, ideas about treatment changed considerably and, as was often the case in Ireland, the Richmond led the way in introducing new therapies for the mentally ill, chiefly in an effort to reduce the frankly disturbing numbers of people in the institutions. This tradition of therapeutic innovation—with all of the benefits and draw-backs of such enthusiasm—had been firmly established when the Richmond opened in the early 1800s, with the explicit goal of implementing 'moral management', the first of many therapeutic paradigms to sweep through the Irish asylums.

## Chapter two

# "Any time they call me, I answer them"

'If a melancholic has been ill
for a year and his case becomes
chronic then the best form of rest
for the mind is often exercise of
the body. It requires a great deal
of discretion as to how this is to
be accomplished, but speaking
on the whole one endeavours to
give them physical work and
light mental work.'

Dr Conolly Norman, RMS, Richmond District Asylum (1905)[1]

From its establishment in 1810, the Richmond pioneered new treatments for lunacy. To begin with, it championed 'moral management', which was defined by Dr Jean-Étienne Dominique Esquirol (1772–1840), a French psychiatrist, as 'the application of the faculty of intelligence and of emotions in the treatment of mental alienation'.[2] This approach represented a significant break from the past, which had emphasised custodial care and control, rather than engagement with each patient as an individual.

Although its precise meaning was rather vague, moral management reflected an important, if incomplete, shift away from traditional treatments such as bloodletting, administration of chemicals and routine confinement, and towards individual patient care.[3] Up to this point, the mentally ill were commonly subjected to restraint in prisons, lunatic wards or private residences, initially involving manacles, hoops, chains and body-straps, with the emphasis moving to straitjackets as the 1800s progressed.[4] Drugs were also used for sedation and chemical restraint: bromides, paraldehyde and chloral.

Moral management sought to reduce or end such practices in the new asylums, and instead recommended a good diet, exercise and occupation, as well as the use of reason and human interaction to effect a cure.[5] To emphasise its commitment to this approach, the Richmond was run by 'moral governors' during the first half of the nineteenth century. These included Richard Grace (1816–30) and, most famously, Samuel Wrigley (1831–57), separated by a brief interlude during which Dr William Heisse (1830–31) ran the asylum.

Speaking with the patient as an individual was central to moral management, a point emphasised by Hallaran in Cork in 1810:

> Maniacs, when in a state to be influenced by moral agents, are not to be subdued *ex officio*, by measures of mere force, and he who will attempt to impose upon their credulity by aiming at too great a refinement in address or intellect, will often find himself detected, and treated by them with marked contempt...I have in consequence made it a special point on my *review days*, to converse for a few minutes with each patient, on the subject which appeared to be most welcome to his humour. By a regular

attention to the duties of this *parade*, I am generally received with as much politeness and decorum as if every individual attached to it, had a share of expectancy from the manner in which he may happen to acquit himself on the occasion. The mental exertion employed amongst the convalescents by this species of address is very remarkable, and the advantages flowing from it are almost incredible.[6]

At the Richmond, Máire A., like many others, presented a challenge to this treatment paradigm during periods when her symptoms were especially intense. Commonly, she would 'hear terrible noises and sounds of feet walking overhead', and become deeply disturbed. According to medical notes:

> There were voices in her head. She got rid of the voices by perseverance and pounding on the bed. People had power to produce this disturbance. They were whispering things into her head. They wanted her to be like themselves but they couldn't get the upper hand of her altogether. She strove to get rid of this annoyance, succeeded to some extent but not entirely. She couldn't see the people who made the noises. Thinks they must have been in hell.

Despite these disturbing experiences and beliefs, the physician still spoke with Máire in some depth and remarked, like Hallaran, on the therapeutic benefits of such conversations, which formed a key component of moral management at the Richmond: 'To my astonishment she concludes one interview by expressing her sense of great and unexpected kindness received, apparently regarding my examinations of her as such'.

Later, Máire reported that 'she never minds the voices now', saying: 'They are leaving my mind'. This improvement was attributed in large part to Máire's participation in occupation at the hospital, another key feature of moral management. Máire was engaged in 'dormitory work', one of a broad array of occupations available as part of asylum treatment.

In 1838 Mollan outlined another case in which appropriate occupation proved central to the patient's recovery:

A man, aged 28, who had served for some years in the East India Company's Artillery, was invalided in the island of St Helena, and discharged as unfit for service in consequence of insanity, which had commenced with delirium tremens [alcohol withdrawal]. He was admitted into the asylum about 12 months after being first attacked [by mental illness], when he was incapable of giving any correct account of himself; he was melancholic, and in general silent; when he did speak, his conversation was an incoherent jumble of the recollection of past events; his general health was a good deal impaired. For nearly three months after his admission there was very little change in his situation, he then began to shew more intelligence, and to take more notice of what was passing around him. It was discovered that he had been accustomed to the care of horses, and was fond of them; advantage was taken of this circumstance, and he was employed about the manager's horse, which in a short time was entrusted entirely to his care. From this period he steadily improved, and his recovery was complete in 12 months from the time of his admission.[7]

The ethics of engaging patients in asylum work without adequate recompense were conveniently side-stepped by regarding occupation as an element of treatment. This particular man, 'after being discharged as a patient', 'was employed as a keeper in the asylum; the duties of which situation he has now performed in a very satisfactory manner for the last two years.' In addition, 'one of the best nurses at present in the establishment is a woman who first entered it as a patient many years ago, and was then in a state of violent excitement'.

Of the 284 patients in the Richmond in 1837, 60 of the men were involved in cultivating the asylum grounds; 15 were engaged in various trades (e.g. tailors, shoemakers, carpenters, weavers); and others were occupied with activities such as making mats and domestic work. Female patients were assigned knitting, spinning, needlework, washing and other domestic tasks. Mollan emphasised that 'small rewards are generally given for the articles manufactured, which here as elsewhere operate powerfully as a stimulus to exertion'.

Mollan was also instrumental in establishing a patients' library in 1844. He became senior physician at the asylum in 1848, following the death of Dr Alexander Jackson.[8]

Mollan's impact on the Richmond was profound. The emphasis he placed on moral management and occupation echoed throughout Ireland's flourishing asylum system for many decades to follow. Older treatments did not, however, disappear entirely. Hydro-therapy, for example, had a long history in psychiatric institutions and 'shower-baths' were commonly used in the Richmond, especially with agitated patients.

Nicholas P. is a good example of someone whose recovery was believed to be dependent on these treatments. Nicholas, a 35-year-old single bootmaker, was committed to the Richmond in 1881 as a 'dangerous lunatic', having 'threatened to take his brother's life with a razor, and also said he would take his own life'. Nicholas was 'intemperate' and had spent ten months in the asylum four years earlier. On this occasion, the doctor recorded that Nicholas 'was very excited and noisy. He speaks of the devil in a very friendly way and he approached me in a violent manner when I said the devil is a bad fellow, which he contradicted and wished me to understand he was no such thing'. The doctor 'ordered him a tepid shower-bath which had a great effect in making him keep himself quiet', although the next day Nicholas told the doctor that he was 'Jesus Christ'. Nicholas remained 'very noisy and talkative' for some time but then showed 'a gradual improvement' and eventually 'lost all delusions'. Nicholas was discharged, 'recovered', after almost eleven months in the Richmond.

Engaging in activities in the asylum was a key element of treatment for all patients, even those with clear symptoms of severe physical and psychiatric illness. Philip B., a 33-year old single pauper (and former clerk), was admitted to the Richmond from South Dublin Union workhouse in the early 1900s, for 'unlawfully' assaulting another inmate. Philip was 'monoplegic' (i.e. had paralysis of a single limb) with marked wasting of the muscles of his right leg, for reasons that were never established. Philip was also, in the words of the admitting doctor, 'suffering from an unlimited supply of delusions'. The doctor recorded Philip's exact words in the clinical file:

> My brains have been removed and other peoples' put in in their place; this was done by two young ladies whom I met one night at the Gaiety Theatre. So, when you have time, doctor, I want you to have my head shaved and the microscope applied so as to find out to whom the brains belong and how much of mine have been removed. I can repeat the Bible from cover to cover and yet have never read a word of it, for Catholics do not read the Bible. Voices speak to me from all quarters and have been transferred [from] the Holy Land to Japan and back.

Three months after admission, Philip remained 'full of delusions of persecution' and believed other people repeated his thoughts. He said 'he was mesmerised on Stephen's Green and knew no more until he found himself here'. Notwithstanding these issues, Philip worked in the 'weaving room' at the Richmond until his transfer to Portrane after just over a year in the Richmond. Two years later, he died in Portrane.

By the start of the twentieth century, occupation had become an especially central element of psychiatric care in Ireland, so that even as other elements of moral management declined in the ever-growing institutions, occupation remained central to the asylums well into the twentieth century. In 1933, Dr Eamonn O'Sullivan established an occupational therapy department in Killarney Mental Hospital and ensured that 85–90 per cent of all patients, including the acutely ill, were involved in special craft centres, re-education therapy classes and recreational treatment centres.[9] Sports, dances and films were encouraged, as well as visits from groups outside the hospital. O'Sullivan's influential 'Textbook of Occupational Therapy with Chief Reference to Psychological Medicine' was published in 1955.[10] Hailed to be the first dedicated text in the world on this subject, the first thousand copies sold out immediately.

Other developments in occupational therapy took place in the Central Criminal Lunatic Asylum in Dundrum,[11] St Patrick's Hospital in Dublin[12] and St Brigid's Mental Hospital in Ballinasloe, where Dr Ada (Adeline) English (1875–1944) introduced multiple progressive reforms, including various sports and occupational therapies.[13] The 1960s saw the emergence of 'industrial therapies' (repetitive, unrewarding work) and a 1961 statutory instrument finally, belatedly and imperfectly addressed the issue of paying patients for work done across all the asylums.[14]

Despite the ostensibly enlightened 'moral management' of the nineteenth century, however, and the 'occupational therapy' of the twentieth century, some patients did not benefit from these approaches and clearly remained troubled or intermittently distressed in the asylums for many decades. Michael R is a good example.

Michael R, a 35-year old student, was committed to the Richmond as a 'dangerous lunatic' in 1881. He was 'astray in his mind' for several years and had 'attempted [to take] the life of his brother with a knife and assaulted him'. On admission to the asylum, Michael said he had 'discovered perpetual motion' and was diagnosed with 'mania'. Over the following years in the Richmond, Michael was generally 'very quiet and contented', although he was 'sometimes very incoherent' and paranoid. After fourteen years in the asylum, he was transferred to Portrane, where he died in 1911. There is no record of Michael receiving any treatment in either asylum at any time.

Not everyone ended up behind asylum walls forever. Occasionally, there were escapes. Richard K., for example, a 27-year old member of the army reserve, was committed to the Richmond as a 'dangerous lunatic' in 1907 because he 'did threaten to take his life'. Admission notes describe Richard as 'very depressed':

> Constable states that patient came to the police station last night and gave himself up, saying that he was going to commit suicide. Today he asked the police to shoot him. Patient is very depressed. He says he is looking for his mother (who is dead). She came to him last night and asked him to go to her. He also hears her voice without seeing her. He has disgraced himself and disgraced all his people.

Two weeks after admission Richard showed 'slight improvement', but over the following months he continued to hear 'two or three voices talking to him at the same time'. After 18 months in the Richmond, however, he was 'cheerful and apparently in good spirits but still hears the voices calling him names'. By this point, Richard was working on the asylum grounds, like a great number of the other male patients.

Three years after admission, Richard was still hearing voices: 'Any time they call me, I answer them', he said. Clinical notes record that 'at times he becomes violent and will strike anyone near him suddenly'. Two months later, while working in the grounds, Richard escaped from the Richmond, and attempts to re-capture him were unsuccessful. Escape was not enormously difficult, especially for those working in the grounds: there were walls, but there was also constant traffic in and out the asylum gates. In his absence, Richard was declared 'discharged, not improved', after three years and two months in the asylum. There is no record of what became of him.

For many, however, there was no escape, or maybe nowhere to escape to. Catherine F., for example, spent decades behind asylum walls with little evidence of either active treatment or therapeutic benefit. Catherine was admitted as a 'dangerous lunatic' in 1885. According to medical notes, she was diagnosed with 'dementia. She threatened to take some people's lives'. The 'supposed cause of insanity' was 'abuse of alcohol'. Following admission, Catherine said that she was 'the Lord and this place is Heaven', and that she 'died of bronchitis before coming here'.

Medical notes record that Catherine saw 'angels all about her. Sometimes there is something wrong with them and they don't know what it is. Sees the Blessed Virgin, St Catherine, St Joseph and St John. Sees saints... some are happy, some not'. Catherine also perceived 'people' who threatened her:

> They threaten to do away with [her]; they threaten her at night; she hears and feels them. She feels one man leaping and prancing inside her. They often get inside her. They are dead. They strive to jump down her throat but are not able to do so. They say wonderful sayings about seeing rats in the room. Asked what place this is, [Catherine] says 'vanished'.

In 1900, fifteen years after admission, Catherine decided 'she is not going to say what talks to her. There are terrible things going on and she does not know what: 'They must be bad spirits'. Medical notes recorded that she 'talks to some imaginary being' and 'hears crying and whinging at night. She thinks the patients here are dead people'. Five years later, Catherine heard 'the voices of dead people' and saw the dead 'all round her'.

'The dead' remained 'very quarrelsome' for Catherine until 1915, some 30 years after admission, when she became 'dull and apathetic', answering 'I don't know' to all questions. Even so, medical notes record that she still 'sees and talks with people who died a hundred years ago and that she constantly sees dead people passing her bed'.

Three decades of institutional life had simply dulled Catherine's symptoms slightly, if at all. Nothing else. Her story presents an important, dispiriting counterpoint to the more positive case histories recounted by Mollan earlier in the nineteenth century. Over the course of the latter half of the century, the asylums had ballooned in size and the enlightened ideals of 'moral management', insofar as they had ever been realised, were greatly diminished. Patients like Michael R. and Catherine F. were deemed 'incurable' and spent their lives in grossly overcrowded, unhygienic asylums, apparently untouched by any treatments provided. Sometimes, their symptoms were blunted by the relentless routines of asylum life, but most continued to suffer intensely. Many, like Máire A. and Catherine F., remained perpetually tormented by voices, visions and dreams of lives they knew they would never lead. Their lives were now 'asylum lives'.

## Chapter three

"I have no home for him. I am sorry for him."

'Mechanical restraint has almost entirely disappeared from modern asylums. I do not use mechanical restraint, but I am not going to lay down any inflexible law. There is more necessity to look after one's patient than to be consistent. I have been in this asylum 20 years and have on two occasions used mechanical restraint.'

Dr Conolly Norman, RMS, Richmond District Asylum (1905)[1]

In mid-1907, Bridget A., a 51-year old 'housewife', was admitted to the Richmond from the North Dublin Union workhouse in a 'very excited' state. Bridget heard voices and believed 'there [was] a plot to kill her'. Six year earlier, Bridget had been living in Dublin's city centre with her husband and children. By 1907, however, she had been 'intemperate for years' and had ended up in the work-house. There was 'no relative present' when she was admitted to the Richmond. Bridget was on her own.

The admitting doctor noted that Bridget's 'mother was eccentric but never in an asylum. She drank'. Bridget, too, admitted that she 'tipples a lot' and this was 'considered the cause of present attack'. In her photograph for the Richmond case-book, Bridget looks considerably older than her 51 years, worn down by a combination of misfortune, alcohol and workhouse life.

On the day of her admission, the doctor noted that Bridget repeatedly 'demands whiskey' and that she now denied being in the workhouse or that 'anyone wanted to hurt her'. Bridget's memory was 'completely gone'. She could not name the date or the month, was confused about how many children she had, and was persistently 'restless and excited'.

A month after admission to the Richmond, Bridget remained confused and 'extremely troublesome, constantly running about the ward interfering with other patients'. When the doctor saw her again in late 1907, the situation had deteriorated further:

> Has been in Padded Room for past few weeks
> till a day or two ago. Is still very restless and
> troublesome, running about and pulling other
> patients about. Rants incoherently and seems
> more or less demented.

The following month, Bridget was described as 'a most irritating old lady, always out of bed and running about the ward, looking for the children, and so on'. Bridget remained 'most incoherent' and 'restless' for the remainder of her time in the asylum, unaware of where she was or how long she had been there. In mid-1909, after spending almost two years in Grangegorman in this disturbed and distressed state, Bridget died there, with 'diabetic coma' (a disorder of blood glucose).

Bridget's complex mix of social problems, physical illness and psychological challenges was typical of people living in the Irish asylums in the early 1900s. By this time, the institutions had expanded, efforts at treatment had declined, and—above all else—the numbers seeking admission kept on rising. In 1844 there were 2,136 'mentally ill' persons resident in public asylums on the island of Ireland; by 1855, this had risen to 3,522; and by 1900, it had reached 16,404.[2] There were also 709 patients in twelve private asylums and four charitable hospitals; 162 patients in the Central Criminal Lunatic Asylum in Dundrum; 89 'lunatics' looked after as single patients in private residences; and 3,805 'mentally ill' residents in workhouses. That came to a total of 21,169 people of whom the majority were in Ireland's 22 district asylums.

All kinds of people were admitted: the mentally ill, the intellectually disabled, the physically ill and people from various other walks of life, who were abandoned or rejected by their communities for any of a wide array of reasons. Many presented for reasons rooted in poverty rather than illness, and some people's problems stemmed entirely from alcohol. Daniel H, for example, a 35-year old married barber with four children, was admitted in the early 1900s owing to being 'violent' and 'refusing to go to bed'. He had 'epilepsy' and was 'intemperate'. Daniel's wife outlined her concerns to the asylum staff in writing:

> Sir,
> Daniel is my husband but is a very cold one. I have not seen him this last three years. I had to leave him all through drink and bring

my four children with me to my mother. [It's been] five years and eight months since he first took those epilepsy fits. Heavy drinking was the cause of them. He never took them when off drink in my presence and in a few days would be at work. I seen him have ten in succession. I am almost certain it is them he has taken now and when in a strange place it will be worse for him...I have no home for him...I am sorry for him.

On admission, Daniel denied all violence and told the doctor he had come to the asylum 'to look for a job at his trade as hairdresser. He cannot tell me why the policeman came with him'. He was 'a very plausible person', according to the clinical file, but his liver was 'enlarged' owing to gross misuse of alcohol.

A week after admission, clinical notes record that Daniel 'seems rather penitent today and blames all his troubles on taking a lot of drink and having no food. He is quite lucid today and states he will take the pledge [not to drink alcohol] and no one will ever see him in an institution like this again'. Daniel remained well over the following weeks and told the doctor that he received a letter from his wife saying she was 'much annoyed at my being here'.

Daniel's wife, however, wrote to the asylum herself to clarify that Daniel should be discharged to the care of his father and sisters and *not* to her. She asked the doctor that 'if you think Daniel is better would you please give him his discharge and let him home [to] his father and sisters...He says he is all right and I am in bad health myself...[He] has a very poor way of doing for the children.'

Daniel was discharged, 'recovered', a few days later, after a month in the Richmond owing entirely to alcohol. Four years later, records indicate that Daniel was working as a labourer, living with his mother, and—tragically—was now a 'widower', his unfortunate wife having succumbed to her 'bad health' in the intervening years.

Alcohol also contributed indirectly to the admission of many other patients, especially women. Around the time that Daniel was committed, Sarah A., a 50-year old widow with five children, was admitted for the third time. She was described as 'intemperate'. At the time of admission, Sarah lived with her widower brother-in-law, his sister-in-law, and his four children, aged between three and 13 years.

Earlier in the day on which she was admitted, Sarah 'tried to throw herself from a top window' because she believed that 'the house was on fire' (it wasn't). On arrival at the asylum, Sarah was bruised and 'restless', with 'delusions of being watched and spied on'. She also 'suffered from worry', 'slight' rheumatism and headaches, and was 'absent minded'. Sarah's 'mother and two sisters' were 'consumptive' (suffered from tuberculosis).

Not only did Sarah herself drink to excess, but she said that her brother-in-law 'takes drink and goes mad through the house all night. He does this three nights a week'. In the photograph in her file, Sarah looks far older than 50: grey hair, downcast eyes, dressed in hospital garb, and clearly worn down by poor physical and mental health and the effects of alcohol on both her and her household. The day after her admission, the doctor recorded that Sarah 'accounts for trying to jump out of the window by saying her nerves were 'out of order'. Questioned about

her brother-in-law, she 'says he threatened her with a knife but denies that this caused her attempt'.

A month after admission, Sarah was 'in bed, looking badly. Very depressed indeed and will hardly speak... Stated to the nurse that she thought she was to be killed but she would not say so to me'. Two months after admission, Sarah remained in this pitiful state: 'Sits all day, looking in front of her, doing nothing. Is very thin and miserable-looking. Does not appear to have actual delusions now but is obviously depressed'.

In December, four months after admission, Sarah was still 'very apathetic. Sits all day, brooding...No interest in anything'. By February 1908, she was 'less depressed' and helped staff around the ward, but had also developed a new symptom:

> She has complained lately of a moving sensation in the epigastrium [just over her stomach]. Thought it was something moving in her, alive. Does not feel it so much these two days.

The next note, in May, recorded some improvement, as Sarah said 'the sensation in her stomach is gone. She supposes it was her nerves. Denies that she now thinks there is a worm there but is reported to believe there is an animal inside her...Helps in ward.'

Sarah, like Daniel and many other patients, was discharged, 'recovered', after some time, but not everyone was this lucky: many patients spent decades behind the asylum walls, sometimes in states of sustained distress that time did not alleviate. In 1918 some 33 years after her admission to the Richmond, Catherine F. was still seeing 'spirits going around the wards' and had 'no idea of time'. According to medical notes:

> She is quiet in the wards but still sees the spirits walking the ward. She told the nurse in charge that she saw one last night shrouded in a sheet walking the ward. These spirits, she contends, never talk to her and generally sit on the ends of other people's beds. She describes them as being animal-like, furnished with claws. Asked if they had a tail, she states 'that is quite possible'.

Soon, Catherine was frankly 'incoherent' and, after 35 years in the Richmond, she eventually died there, with 'fatty degeneration of the heart'.

Catherine's fate was not uncommon: lengthy institutionalisation, persistent symptoms, and death inside the asylum walls. Most of Catherine's life was indelibly shaped by the Richmond, its rules and regulations, its character and context. What kind of life did Catherine lead? What was it like to live inside the Richmond in the nineteenth and early twentieth centuries?

Asylum life was highly regulated. The 1903 'Regulations for the Management of the Richmond District Asylum' laid out some general if idealistic principles for managing patients such as Catherine, emphasising the need to avoid both cruelty and neglect:

> With regard to the general treatment of the inmates it is to be remembered that the patients

are all persons under hospital treatment for the cure or care of a diseased condition. They are, therefore, to be treated with the utmost consideration, every care being taken to study their cases with a view to cure where that is possible and to the amelioration of their condition. Cruelty to patients will under no circumstances be tolerated, and it must be remembered that neglect of those who are unable to look after themselves is equivalent to cruelty. No effort must be spared to endeavour to occupy patients who are convalescent or those whose physical condition fits them for occupation.[3]

There were particular regulations governing 'restraints', such as straitjackets, which could only be used 'by recorded order of one or more of the medical officers' and if 'necessary for purposes of surgical or medical treatment, or to prevent the patient injuring himself, or herself, or others'.[4] In 1905, Dr Conolly Norman, Resident Medical Superintendent from 1886 to 1908, duly reported that restraint was very rarely used at the Richmond during his time there. Even if this was true (and it is debatable, to say the least), asylum life was still very harsh: patients slept in large crowded wards with primitive bedding rather than bedsteads; there was no privacy; communal bathrooms were the norm; and patients held no personal possessions: clothes, spectacles and even dentures were common property, randomly allocated each day.

Other measures in the 1903 regulations governed the bewildering array of staff members in the institution:

medical officers, nurses, attendants, servants, laundresses, cooks, craftsmen, gardeners, and household staff. The Richmond was, like all asylums, a very busy place. There were hundreds of staff members coming and going, frequent discharges and (especially) admissions, and a steady stream of tradespersons, visitors, inspectors and assorted others passing in and out through the asylum gates. The 1903 regulations addressed the issue of visitors to patients in some detail, noting that 'with the permission of the RMS, patients may be visited by their friends on such days and at such hours as may be fixed by him and approved by the Joint Committee'.[5] For some, however, visits were not without complexity, owing to the patients' mental states.

Helena B., for example, a 27-year old single 'servant', was admitted as a 'dangerous lunatic' in the mid-1880s having 'assaulted her mother'. Helena had a 'fair' degree of education and had been 'confined previously in Richmond Asylum'. Helena stated that 'she was sent here because she used to curse and call names'. She said she 'was a child of Mary' and that 'her reported mother was not her mother, but a woman in charge of her'. Helena was 'very incoherent', 'somewhat hypochondriacal', and stated that 'the public suppression of intemperance has me here'.

Medical notes from 1901, over a decade since her admission, record that Helena's 'brother came to see her 10 or 11 years ago' and 'she has not seen him since'. She was worried something had happened to her brother, although 'a plump lump of a man (really her brother) came to see her who (she says) is not her brother'. Helena had delusions that people she knew (including her brother) had been replaced by doubles, a syndrome later known as Capgras Syndrome, after Joseph Capgras (1873–1950), a

French psychiatrist who described this unusual disorder in 1923.

For Helena and her fellow patients, the Richmond sought to provide a range of occupational pursuits to alleviate symptoms such as these or at least provide an alternative focus for patients' energy and attention. In 1838, Mollan reported that such activities benefitted both the physical *and* mental health of all patients, especially the 'incurable':

> The general health is promoted, discipline is maintained, and active exertion in the open air is found more advantageous in producing quiet sleep than opiates. Many of our most industrious patients are persons whose cases are likely to prove incurable, but who are made as happy as their several states admit of; some, by their labours, are fully requiting, others materially lessening the expense of their maintenance to the public.[6]

Patient labour certainly lessened asylum expenses considerably, as Mollan reported that 'all the clothing for both males and females is made up by the patients, with the exception of hats and shoes'. In 1838, '2,088 yards of linen and calico were woven in the establishment, the yarn for the linen having been spun by the females, and 524 pairs of stockings were made by them':

> Of the advantages of this system of employment, I can speak in very decided terms; persons who, when unemployed, are noisy,

violent in their demeanor, quarrelsome, and discontented, very generally become, under the influence of suitable occupation, tranquil, orderly, and easily managed; and to its salutary effects I mainly attribute the recovery of numerous cases, some of which were at first most unpromising...I can confidently say, that at least eight out of every ten lunatics will be found in a fit state for some useful pursuit.

Leisure activities included musical concerts, recitals, visits from drama groups, and reading, for those who were literate, in the patients' library, which Mollan was instrumental in establishing in 1844. Mollan's successor, Dr Joseph Lalor, served as RMS from 1857 to 1886, and paid particular attention to developing the Richmond school, which taught patients a range of subjects, including reading, writing, arithmetic, algebra, geometry, geography, drawing, needlework and various arts and crafts.

The asylum school was a highly progressive feature of the asylum, not least because it was developed at the same time that Ireland's general education system was just finding its feet. In 1831, a decision was taken to establish a national system of education in Ireland in order to socialise the Irish population, strengthen Ireland's links with the British Empire, and address the poverty and limited prospects of the Irish.[7] Teachers were trained and Commissioners of National Education approved and produced textbooks for use in schools. Despite this flurry of activity, however, only 36% of children attended school regularly in 1870, owing chiefly to the difficult socio-economic circumstances of the country.

In the Richmond, Lalor considered education to be the very basis of moral treatment of the insane and it became a defining feature of asylum life during this period.[8] By 1878, 400 of the Richmond's 479 male patients, and 448 of its 553 female patients, were either attending the school or engaged in occupation. Most of those who were neither attending the school nor occupationally engaged were too physically unwell to do so; few were absent owing to their mental state. The Richmond school attracted attention from far and wide, with the renowned Dr Daniel Hack Tuke (1827–95) singling it out for particular praise in the *Journal of Mental Science* in 1875.[9]

Sport was another important feature of asylum life, aimed at relieving the 'gloomy monotony' and encouraging patients to become more active in athletics, cricket and various other activities. Staff, too, were involved and none more so than Dr Daniel Frederick Rambaut.[10] Rambaut promoted occupational therapy in the institution and was an especially keen sportsman, playing rugby internationally for Ireland in the 1880s.[11] In the asylums, sport could serve as an important leveller when both patients and staff participated, in a rare but not unique relaxation of hospital hierarchy.[12]

As pathologist to the Richmond, the multi-talented Rambaut was also involved in one of the most interesting, puzzling controversies in the history of the establishment: the outbreak of a mysterious malady among patients and staff who fell ill with the same affliction in the mid-1890s and some of whom died. This was a medical mystery that occupied the attention of asylum staff for several frustrating years as the nineteenth century drew to a close. In the end, the problem seemed to lie with the asylum diet.

## Chapter four

# "The melancholic wastes even if he is fed abundantly."

# 'The first reason why you should send a patient to an asylum is refusing food. The second reason is self-mutilation.'

Dr Conolly Norman, RMS, Richmond District Asylum (1906)[1]

Food was a hugely important aspect of life in the Irish asylums. Food supplies were documented in obsessional detail and patients' diets carefully monitored and regulated. Failure to eat and weight loss were associated with mental illness, while a good appetite and weight gain indicated recovery. In 1905 Conolly Norman outlined some of the ways in which mental illness was linked with a person's diet:

> Some patients refuse food because they desire to fast. Their wish is to mortify themselves. Our patient here refused his food because the sins at which he hinted, which he believed destroyed his soul, were sins of a nature which perhaps it might be deemed that fasting and abstinence might be appropriate for. Another reason often assigned is that the patient is too wicked to live, or desires to die, and he refuses food with the design of destroying himself... Sometimes patients say they have taken too much food, and won't take any more. It has

done them physical harm...Sometimes they refuse food because it is poisoned, or as they say, 'There is something in it', meaning that it is poisoned...There is a rather important group of patients who are stubborn and refuse food in obedience to a Divine command'.[2]

The Irish asylums were established and operated during the nineteenth century, when food was often scarce in Ireland. The Great Famine saw the Irish population fall by approximately 20 per cent between 1845 and 1852. Over one million people died and another million emigrated in the immediate aftermath. The Famine, and how it is imaged and remembered, are key elements of Irish history and identity.[3]

The Famine did not have a dramatic impact on admission rates to the asylums because admissions were rising increasingly rapidly during this period anyway.[4] Asylum beds were filled as soon as they opened, so the limiting factor was the supply of beds rather than demand for admission. Even so, after the Famine there was an 86 per cent increase in *first* admissions for severe mental illness, especially between 1860 and 1875, when babies conceived during the Famine reached the high-risk age for what is now known as schizophrenia. This led the Inspectors of Lunatics to speculate that 'children born and partially reared amidst the horrors of the famine and the epidemics of disease that followed it were so handicapped in their nervous equipment as to be weak minded from the start or to fall victims to mental disease later'.[5]

The Famine might also have had longer-term, transgenerational effects, which are only now being considered.[6] More specifically, it seems possible that inherited changes in how genes are expressed, rather than changes in genes themselves (i.e. 'epigenetic effects'), resulting from the Famine, might have passed on experiences of physical and psychological trauma to subsequent generations in a lasting, biological way. Intriguing as it is, this hypothesis requires greater study prior to further speculation.[7]

Throughout the nineteenth century, the advent of the Famine and shortages of food underlined the importance that the Richmond traditionally attached to diet and appetite as indicators of illness or recovery, and to food as a mechanism of treatment, even when it clearly made no difference to the outcome. Charles P., for example, was a 30-year-old single man admitted to the Richmond in the early 1880s with 'alcoholism' and 'confusion of mind', apparently owing to syphilis, a sexually transmitted infection that commonly affected the brain. Charles was 'very restless' and 'constantly undressing himself'.

In the absence of antibiotics, the chief treatment for Charles was dietary: milk and beef tea. Perhaps unsurprisingly, Charles remained in a dreadful state, 'refusing food', seeing 'imaginary objects', and showing 'dread and fear' of everything. Soon, he was 'suffering from profound exhaustion' and 'completely demented'. Charles 'died in epileptic fit' in the asylum, a direct result of syphilis and alcohol misuse, in the absence of any treatment for his condition—apart from ineffective dietary measures.

As well as being seen as a treatment, food was also an important way to exercise visible, institutional control over patients. Regulations at the Richmond specified that 'the hours of meals shall be fixed by the RMS [Resident Medical Superintendent], with the sanction of the Joint Committee'.[8] In 1862, patients' breakfast comprised one quart of 'stirabout' (oatmeal porridge), one pint of milk or tea, and half a pound of bread.[9] Dinner was half a pound of meat, one pint of soup and bread (10 ounces for a male, eight ounces for a female). Supper comprised a pint of cocoa and half a pound of bread. For patients on 'extras', there were eggs at breakfast, a pint of beer or porter at dinner, and half a pound of chops (meat), half a chicken, or a pint of beef tea (made with stewed extract of beef). Food was served in vast dining halls, and selected patients assisted staff in the preparation of industrial quantities of food for meals.

For additional dietary treatment, medical officers could order tea for supper for certain patients, as well as a 'hospital diet' with extra portions of regular foods as well as rice, whiskey and arrowroot (a starch-based foodstuff, common in asylums). Helena B. is a good example for the use of diet for treatment in this way. Like Charles P., Helena B. was admitted in the 1880s with 'dementia' (a general, catch-all diagnosis). On admission, Helena had a murmur in her heart ('mitral presystolic murmur') and signs of lung disease, possibly tuberculosis ('shade of dullness, left [lung] apex'). Perhaps predictably, the much-afflicted Helena did not do well during her protracted stay in the asylum. By 1902, almost two decades after admission, Helena had become 'weak-minded and delusional', and 'irritable at times'. According to medical notes, she tended to sit 'up in bed cursing and talking to herself during the day and at night'.

Clearly unwell, Helena was put on an 'extra diet' of '2 oz whiskey' and an egg each day. Notwithstanding these measures, Helena died the following year, of 'valvular disease of the heart'. Helena's 'extra diet' was clearly insufficient to remedy her long-standing heart disease, her probable tuberculosis, or the vicissitudes of asylum life which, in Helena's case, also included an apparent episode of 'beri beri', which had left her heartbeat 'extremely irregular' in its aftermath.

The story of 'beri beri' at the Richmond is an interesting, puzzling and important one for the asylum and its history. During the summer of 1894, several patients developed a mysterious illness that proved fatal for some and appeared—as best as anyone could tell—to involve inflammation of the nerves. RMS Conolly Norman consulted widely about the possible cause of the malady, even seeking the advice of Sir William Thornley Stoker (1845–1912), prominent surgeon, president of the Royal College of Surgeons in Ireland (1896) and brother of Bram, author of *Dracula* (1897).[10]

The mysterious illness certainly required urgent attention from the leading medical minds of the day. Between June 1894 and 1898, 546 patients and staff at the Richmond developed the disorder, and 10 per cent of those affected died.[11] In 1896, Dr Rambaut, the hospital pathologist, was sent to examine some seamen who exhibited similar symptoms, which can include difficulties walking, numbness in the hands and feet, pain, confusion, speech difficulties and vomiting, as well as a range of cardiac symptoms, such as increased heart rate and shortness of breath on exertion. Rambaut concluded that their cases closely resembled those seen at the Richmond. As a result, it was decided—rightly or wrongly—that the asylum diet (low in fruit and vegetables, high in white bread) had led to beri beri,[12] a condition caused chiefly by a nutritional deficit in vitamin B1 (thiamine).

This diagnosis was not, however, without its critics. The ever-flexible Rambaut translated the report of two Dutch physicians who spent six days at the Richmond in 1897 looking into the issue. The Dutch doctors concluded that there was, in fact, no difficulty with the diet at the institution and they cast serious doubt on the diagnosis of beri beri. Nevertheless, Norman wrote in 1899 that asylums seemed especially prone to outbreaks of beri beri and that the condition appeared to be more common in patients with epilepsy compared to those without.[13]

But all kinds of patients were affected, not just those with epilepsy. In the mid-1880s, for example, William M., a 44-year-old single labourer, was committed to the Richmond as a 'dangerous lunatic'. He was described as 'intemperate', 'violent', 'rambling and incoherent in manner'. He was deemed 'likely to do bodily harm to himself and others' and diagnosed as 'probably a case of amentia' (severe intellectual disability). 'Weak-minded since birth', William reportedly had a 'crass, childish face'; 'his nostrils [were] wide and his nose flat and broad'; and his 'palate very highly arched'—all of which suggested intellectual disability rather than mental illness.

In the Richmond, William was 'very silent and uncommunicative' and had 'no idea of the time'. In his hometown, William 'was always looked upon as a village idiot who had sunk in social grade much below his immediate relatives'. Unfortunately, William developed beri beri in the Richmond in 1896 and, like many others, was promptly transferred to Portrane for further care. There is no further record of William's progress there, but having spent 12 years behind asylum walls by the time of his transfer, the overwhelming likelihood is that William died in Portrane, beri beri being just one of the many factors shaping his tragic life behind asylum walls.

Despite the considerable attention paid to the issue at the time, the nature of the illness that struck the Richmond in the 1890s remains unclear today. Crawford notes that, based on a nutritional analysis of the Richmond diet, an outbreak of beri beri seems unlikely—just as the Dutch physicians concluded at the time.[14] Other possibilities include the effects of some of the medications used for the treatment of epilepsy, such as drugs based on bromide salts, but the matter might never be fully resolved.

What is clear, however, is that this mysterious affliction affected the lives of many of the Richmond's patients in different ways over many years, and highlighted the importance of ensuring good nutritional content in asylum food.[15] By 1916, the 'Vegetables Issued' book at the asylum listed a wide variety of vegetables that were available at that point, ranging from asparagus to seakale, from leeks to spinach.[16] The most commonly issued vegetables and herbs were cabbage, onions, parsley, thyme, cauliflower, celery and turnips, although the quantities of these healthy foodstuffs were never sufficient for the hospital's enormous population.

Ellen B. is a good example of someone for whom the combinations of illnesses and challenges that asylum patients commonly experienced were compounded by bad diet. A 35-year-old single 'worker', Ellen was admitted to the Richmond as a 'dangerous lunatic' in 1885, having previously been in an asylum in 1871, for nine months. Ellen was Roman Catholic, could read and write, and the 'supposed cause' of her insanity was 'religion'. According to medical notes, Ellen had 'attempted to throw herself out of a window'. Even so, Ellen was 'cheerful' on admission although her remote memory was 'bad'.

During her 17 years in the Richmond, Ellen developed not only beri beri but also lung disease (most likely tuberculosis contracted within the institution) and 'threatened cardiac failure'. Mentally, she slipped into a state of 'profound weakmindedness with impairment of memory' over time. According to medical notes, Ellen knew neither where she was nor how long she had been there. But she was generally 'harmless' and often 'cheery', despite her multiple ailments and misfortunes.

In addition to the 10 per cent mortality associated with beri beri, Ellen's lung disease presented a real and urgent risk to her life, a risk exacerbated by the poor diet and unhygienic living conditions of the Richmond. In 1905 the ever-prescient Norman highlighted pulmonary tuberculosis ('phthisis') as directly linked with weight loss, and a key issue in the institution:

> The melancholic wastes even if he is fed abundantly, and the anergic chap gets fat if attended to in this way. It is natural that the melancholic who wastes his little powers and is subject to perpetual anguish of mind should waste away physically even when getting plenty of food. It is probable that all his organic functions are more or less interfered with. Even anergic people will waste, lose substance, lose colour. Stuperose cases tend to physical trouble in a special way. Their breathing is shallow. They don't take exercise except forced, and phthisis occurs in the apices of the lungs, the portions least expanded which are most open to attack. So, our people who will not breathe properly,

will not open the lungs, are particularly liable to phthisis'.[17]

As a result of all of these factors—pre-existing illness, psychiatric disturbance over many years, poor diet, unhygienic living conditions, and limited medical care—tuberculosis was soon the leading cause of death among asylum patients in the Richmond and elsewhere. There was especially high mortality among patients who presented to the asylum with established physical illnesses and then refused to eat in the Richmond, leading, in many cases, to force-feeding in a desperate effort to improve their nutrition. Eliza H. is a good, if disturbing, example.

Eliza, a 46-year-old 'labourer's wife', was admitted to the asylum in early 1908. Admission notes record a six-day history of 'persecutory delusions' (paranoia) and hearing 'people calling her bad names' (auditory hallucinations). Eliza's education was recorded as 'none'; she was 'temperate' (i.e. did not misuse alcohol); and this was her 'first attack'.

On physical examination, Eliza was 'anaemic' (pale) and there was evidence of serious problems with two of the valves in her heart: one was too narrow ('mitral stenosis') and another was incompetent ('aortic regurgitation' with 'visible pulsation'). Clinical notes record that Eliza had been 'in Baggot Street Hospital for nine days with her heart. She became noisy [and] refused her food there at times'.

On arrival at Grangegorman, Eliza also had 'blepharitis' (inflammation of the eyelids) and told the doctor that 'she saw something going round her eyes'. While her speech was slow and 'incoherent at times', Eliza managed to complain quite clearly about the staff and other patients in the asylum:

The people in the ward are all going about
snuffing and snuffing at me. They called me
filthy names. I don't care. I'm not a bad woman.
The nurse was one of them.

The morning after admission, Eliza 'refused her breakfast', lay down with her eyes closed, and would not talk to
staff. As was customary in the asylum, she was force-fed
through a nasal tube. As a result, she became 'very agitated and troublesome and [was] put in padded room in
consequence'. Eliza continued to refuse to speak with the
doctor over the following days.

After two weeks in Grangegorman, the doctor recorded
that Eliza was 'very weakly, speech indistinct. Does not
know me or where she is...Moved out of padded room'.
A week later, after just three weeks in the asylum, Eliza
died of 'exhaustion from acute melancholia'. Most clinical
files at Grangegorman contain a photograph of the patient
but Eliza's does not. Instead, there is a hand-written note:
'Died—too restless for photo'.

Notwithstanding efforts to improve diet and even
force-feed patients like Eliza, thousands of patients died
in the institutions throughout the nineteenth and early
twentieth centuries.

## Chapter five

"I am doomed to live this unfortunate life of mine forever."

# 'You cannot allow a patient to go about at large distraining his property or making a fool of himself. You must give them asylum treatment. Besides, it gives a man the best chance of recovery.'

Dr Conolly Norman, RMS, Richmond District Asylum (1905)[1]

Ellen B., admitted to the Richmond as a 'dangerous lunatic' in 1885, had a multitude of problems during her time there: beri beri, lung disease and 'threatened cardiac failure', as well as 'mania' and being 'suicidal, at times very violent'. A medical note in 1899 reported that she 'talks away rapidly to herself'. She remained, after 14 years in the asylum, in a state of 'excitement'.

In 1901, Ellen told her doctor she was 'dying with fits about which you know nothing'. The following year, she was 'markedly incoherent and babbles a good deal'. At this point, Ellen was transferred to the branch asylum in Portrane, north Dublin. As Ellen had already spent some seventeen years behind asylum walls, the overwhelming likelihood is that she died in Portrane: once a person was detained in an Irish asylum for more than five years, it was almost inevitable that they would die there.[2]

Even so, Norman's rather bright-eyed enthusiasm about 'recovery' at the Richmond was not entirely without basis. Of the 608 patients admitted between January 1833 and December 1837, over half were discharged, 'recovered' or 'relieved' by 1838, although one in seven died.[3] The rate of admission during this period, at 122 per annum, increased to 158 by 1862.[4] In that year, just over half of all admissions (54 per cent) were of women, and the most common diagnosis was 'mania' (61 per cent) followed by 'melancholia' (16 per cent), 'monomania' (a single, focused delusion; 11 per cent), 'dementia' (a broad, catch-all term; 10 per cent) and 'idiocy' (1 per cent).

Despite the apparently high discharge rate, 'incurable' lunatics accumulated in the asylums, contributing significantly to chronic overcrowding. By 1862, there were 678 patients in the Richmond of whom over three quarters (515 patients) were 'lunatics probably incurable'. The remainder were 'lunatics probably curable' (14 per cent), 'epileptics' (7 per cent) and 'idiots' (2 per cent). A majority were either 'quiet and orderly, but insane' (46 per cent) or 'moderately tranquil' (39 per cent), but a significant minority were 'noisy and refractory' (12 per cent) and a small number were 'convalescent' (3 per cent).

The most common cause of death among men in the Richmond in the 1830s was 'inflammation of brain or its membranes' and in women was 'phthisis' (pulmonary tuberculosis).[5] Other contributors to the high mortality rate included 'paralysis', 'pneumonia', 'fever', 'old age and general debility'. By 1862, 'phthisis' had become the most common cause of death, with significant numbers of others dying of 'bronchitis', 'paralysis', 'exhaustion' and 'diarrhoea'—much of which was directly attributable to the overcrowded, unhygienic condition of the asylum.[6]

It is highly probable that Ellen B. died of tuberculosis in Portrane. Tuberculosis was a particular problem in nineteenth and early twentieth-century Ireland, both inside and outside the institutions. In the early 1900s, tuberculosis accounted for almost 16 per cent of all deaths in the Irish general population and 25 per cent of asylum deaths, with an average age of death of between 37 and 39 years.[7] There were similar problems with tuberculosis in asylums in other jurisdictions owing to their size and the unhygienic conditions that prevailed.

Other infections also occurred and commonly claimed lives. Martin P., a 50-year-old married porter, was committed to the Richmond in 1884 as a 'dangerous lunatic' having been 'five days ill and violent'. He was diagnosed with 'mania' owing to 'softening of the brain'. Admission notes record that Martin 'has lost his speech since Sunday last' and 'refuses to take food'. He was 'likely to do bodily harm to himself and others if not put under proper restraint'. Asking for a knife, Martin 'stated that he hoped God would prevent him from committing suicide'.

According to his clinical file, Martin 'was a case of dementia complicated with a very unusual disease, diphtheria', which is an infection that presents with a sore throat and fever—and can prove fatal if untreated. Martin had a high temperature and 'was in a very collapsed state' on admission to the Richmond. He was 'at once put on milk, brandy, eggs and beef tea', his 'throat swabbed with sulphuric acid', and he was 'isolated from the rest of the patients'.

Despite these measures, Martin deteriorated rapidly. Four days after admission he was much worse, refusing all food and being 'fed with tube three times a day' (i.e.

force-fed). Martin died two days later, from 'exhaustion and paralysis of the muscles of deglutition' (swallowing), as a result of diphtheria. Today, diphtheria is preventable by vaccination, but in the nineteenth century it commonly led to death through paralysis of the muscles of the throat. Martin never stood a chance.

Heart disease was another common illness in the asylums and accounted for the deaths of Máire A., Catherine F. ('fatty degeneration of the heart') and Helena B. ('valvular disease of the heart'). Post-mortems were commonly performed in order to elucidate precise causes of death, which were then tabulated carefully and reported annually, although little was actually done to address these causes. Some patients had such complicated combinations of physical and mental illness that no clear cause of death could be selected from the many possibilities. This was especially true for older adults like Annie C.

A 75-year-old married woman, Annie C. was admitted to the Richmond in 1907, from the North Dublin Union workhouse. Admission notes record that Annie would 'answer no questions. Tries to escape...Continually throws herself out of bed'. As a result, Annie had multiple bruises all over her body and possibly a fractured rib.

On admission, Annie was both mentally and physically ill in multiple different ways. She had swelling of her left foot, abnormal chest sounds (suggesting possible bronchitis or a chest infection), a curved spine and an opacity in one of her eyes—likely a cataract. She was profoundly disoriented and did not know the ages of her children. Annie claimed to have seen her husband the previous day when he was, in fact, far away in another hospital. For the photograph in her file, a staff member had to hold Annie's head upright and, even then, Annie looked away, restless and distracted.

Annie was diagnosed with senile dementia and, a week after admission, remained 'restless' and confused: 'Asked her age, says that is a hard thing to answer. Asked is she 15, says, "Oh, yes". 20? "Yes". 30? "I think so". 40? "Oh no!" She draws the line at 30, evidently'.

A month after admission, Annie claimed that her name was 'Bridget Ryan' and she was '26 years old'. She seemed to be losing weight but, according to the notes, was 'too frail to weigh'. The following month, November 1907, Annie deteriorated further and was now 'very frail and quite demented'. She continued to decline rapidly and—inevitably—died in the asylum in 1908. Annie's cause of death was listed as 'chronic enteritis', a rather non-specific diagnosis linked with presumed inflammation of the intestine. In truth, the cause of Annie's death is unknown and was possibly unknowable.

In addition to physical illnesses, many asylum patients experienced sustained psychiatric or psychological symptoms during their time inside. Máire A. had persistent 'melancholia' for many years and heard 'terrible noises', with people 'whispering things into her head'. Catherine F. saw 'angels all around her' and heard and felt dead people 'inside her'. Helena B. was 'weak-minded and delusional', sitting up in bed 'cursing and talking to herself during the day and at night'. And Ellen B. had 'mania' and was 'suicidal' and, 'at times, very violent'.

In a similar vein, Timothy W., a 23-year-old single assistant teacher, was admitted in the early 1900s with a three-day history of being 'noisy, shouting and singing'. He believed that 'his soul was lost'. On arrival in the asylum, Timothy was 'in a semi-stuperose state', sitting 'in a fixed attitude in his chair', answering questions only 'at long intervals'. He admitted hearing voices but would not provide details.

A week after admission, Timothy remained very unwell, 'in a rather restless state. He assumes all kinds of dramatic gestures and poses, and addressed me: "How now...What would'st thou with me?" Then he closed his fists and assumed a pugilistic attitude'. Timothy retained a rather grandiose tone over the following weeks, saying to the doctor that:

> I would feign bless thee and respect thee. I see a bell. I would like to ring it. I look at pictures on the wall. I would like to spit but far be it from me to do so. I am inclined to take a chair and throw it through the window.

This kind of disordered thought and behaviour intensified to the extent that Timothy was soon 'confined to a single room' and was 'very noisy and restless', 'always talking to himself':

> He seems fond of striking attitudes and a favourite one of his is to arrange a blanket on him like the old Roman dress and to make gestures as if he were making a speech. He is consistently chattering but I cannot distinguish what he says.

In light of Timothy's ongoing symptoms, he was assigned extra rations: 'four ounces of whiskey, four eggs,

and four milk'. Three months after admission, Timothy declared himself 'very well' and, three months later again, his doctors agreed he was 'much improved', although 'this morning he sang aloud at the top of his voice a psalm in Latin'. In addition, the doctor chose not to post a letter that Timothy wrote (the intended recipient is not known):

> My Dear Sir,
> 'Man proposes but God disposes'.[8] I must from this day cease correspondence with people I know not.
>
> This is the mighty Kingdom of Purgatory where a man has to lead a life as pure as a 'Dove' in order to fit him for the City outside these walls.
>
> I dined, knelt, taught and prayed with people both belonging (and not belonging) to the order in which I am enrolled in 'K.B.' A true Roman Catholic, I have my duty to fulfil towards my 'God' and I am sure the Day shall come when I may be high in his estimation and in the estimation of others as well.
>
> If I am selected to be a 'Teacher' I shall do my endeavour to love my 'Pupils'...If the laws permit otherwise, faithfully shall I work in the garden. I both forgive and forget the injustice I done on the gentlemen inside these walls, and ask all to join hands and be friends once more. 'Ecce quam bonum et quam iucundum habitare fratres in unum'.[9]
>
> If the rules of such a school point out to me to teach Christian Doctrine, faithfully shall

I fulfil my Duty. As regards other subjects, I have learned 'something of everything and everything of something'.[10] English is my best subject. Arithmetic and algebra can I teach. Drawing, astronomy, French, Irish, Latin and science am I well acquainted with.

I shall do my endeavour to treat the children with kindness and consideration, and encourage them to persevere and the lowly child as well as the highly. If such be the will of the just one that I shall get cash, forget them at Xmas I shall not. A book prize shall I give in preference to cash. My heart is longing to be with children...Vows I have taken to lead a 'pure life', abstain from drink, smoking and night-walking...

Wishing all a happy Christmas,

I remain your most obedient servant in Jesus Christ...'

After nine months in the Richmond, Timothy was still hearing voices but was 'quiet and well behaved'. A year after admission, he was 'much improved' and recognised 'that he was insane'. He still had some symptoms, telling the doctor that he heard the voice of a boy he once knew the previous night, and 'just now, as you spoke, I saw his vision opposite to me'. Notwithstanding this, Timothy was discharged, 'recovered', as the doctor chose to overlook his clear and persisting symptoms in order to release him from the asylum.

Patients who presented with suicidality were also quite commonly discharged, especially if there were few other symptoms of mental illness. Around the same time Timothy W. was admitted, Denis R., a 36-year-old single labourer, was transferred from nearby Mountjoy Prison. Two weeks earlier, Denis had stopped a passer-by on South Great George's street in Dublin and asked him to sharpen a small table knife. The passer-by thought the request strange so he followed Denis and soon saw Denis draw the knife across his throat.

A constable was called and, along with more passers-by, overpowered Denis, who was now bleeding from the throat. They brought him to Mercer's Hospital, where it was determined that his injuries were not serious. Denis was then brought to College Street police station and charged with attempting suicide. Denis commented to the passer-by: 'If you had sharpened the knife, it would be all over now'.

Clinical notes from the Richmond record that, some days after the incident, Denis was 'committed to Mountjoy Prison...under sentence of one calendar month for attempted suicide. He was very excitable in prison... shouting out at intervals'. He had been 'drinking on and off till his arrest'. Speaking with the doctor, Denis denied attempting suicide, but said he would like to do so in the future: 'As sure as God is in heaven, I would'. Denis had had a number of previous admissions to the Richmond and had a brother in the asylum in Portrane, with epilepsy.

A week after admission, Denis finally admitted to his suicide attempt and described hearing voices in the context of drink:

> I attempted suicide because I was out of my mind and I would do the same at present. I

heard Captain Stewart and Captain Crawford talking about me: 'We have him now and we will hold him'.

A week later, Denis reported that he 'had great comfort' the previous two nights because 'the captains were not speaking to me at all'. That remained the case for the rest of Denis's time in the Richmond, as he admitted that 'it was all on account of the drink and as long as he keeps off the drink he knows he will be all right'. Denis was discharged, 'recovered', after five months in Grangegorman.

Other patients were admitted with relatively clear cases of depression or 'melancholia', and also discharged. Elizabeth A., a 22-year-old dress-maker, was admitted in 1907 because she was 'depressed. Thinks her soul is lost. Thinks she changed her life from what it used to be. Kept awake always thinking about her soul'. Elizabeth said her 'mind was tortured' and 'this tormented her father with her sufficiently in the last two or three months till he had to send her here'. In her photograph, Elizabeth looks directly into the camera, her complexion dark, her eyes untrusting.

A week after admission, Elizabeth denied 'thinking her soul is lost but admits she <u>did</u> think so for two months'. Just three weeks later, Elizabeth was again 'extremely depressed. Says her soul is lost and she is going to die... I cannot get any more definite reason for this feeling than that she used to annoy her father'. The following month, Elizabeth spoke little to the doctor:

> Patient very quiet and depressed. She says her
> soul is lost but will give no reason for so think-
> ing. When talking she turned away from me

and did not look at me. When I asked her to turn around, she would not talk again to me.

The following month, Elizabeth was 'extremely depressed' and spoke 'only in a whisper'. She was wracked with guilt, saying 'she would strangle herself' owing to 'the way in which I left my father. I used to be roaring and keeping him awake'. She told the doctor that 'she was "struck by the Hand of God" on account of the way she went on':

> Asked how she 'went on', says a priest she was in the habit of going to went away for a time and told her not to go to any other priest in his absence, but she did go and considers her soul is lost in consequence.

By February 1908 Elizabeth was finally improving and in May she told the doctor that 'I thought my soul was gone but I think it's alright again'. By August she was 'rather brighter' and said that 'her mind was upset when she thought' her 'soul was lost'. Elizabeth was discharged, 'recovered' in late 1908, after 14 months in Grangegorman.

Other patients were discharged relatively promptly, chiefly because there was never anything wrong with them in the first place. Hanora M., admitted in the early 1900s, was a 32-year-old 'prostitute' transferred from Mountjoy Prison. Hanora had been admitted to the asylum 'frequently' in the past. She was described as 'intemperate' and her religion recorded as 'nil'. On this occasion, Hanora was admitted for being 'excitable' in prison, leading to 'violence, assaults on officers'. Physical examination was normal, apart from an old fracture of her left clavicle (collar bone).

Clinical notes record that Hanora was, 'as usual, flippant, truculent and inclined to be abusive'. She 'says if she had known they were sending her back here, she would have done for one of the matrons this morning'. Hanora was 'extremely abusive towards the nurses', telling the doctor that 'she should be locked up in a cell and not left to be murdered by those whores'. In her photograph, Hanora wears a dark shawl and has the stoic expression of a person long accustomed to institutions.

The following week, Hanora explained to the doctor that a fortnight after her most recent discharge from the asylum, 'she was arrested for soliciting. Every policeman has to have seven prisoners in the month...[I] didn't do anything'. After two weeks in the asylum, even the doctor had to admit that Hanora 'appears quite sane. But, of course, she is liable to get into a violent temper and break out any minute'. After another fortnight, Hanora was still 'quiet, but I can see she is holding herself in with an effort. She says that we should not take her in when they send her from prison, and contradicts me when I assure her we must do so'.

In January 1908, after two months in Grangegorman, Hanora remained 'lucid' but had been involved in a fracas with another patient, whom Hanora said 'struck her'. In early February, Hanora was 'quiet, lucid, coherent'. She was also 'impudent and full of ill-feeling to everyone here, but at the same time is probably as well as she ever will be'. Hanora was discharged, 'recovered', having spent three months in the asylum for no identifiable reason, apart from allegedly being a 'prostitute' and being truculent in prison.

Even among those who appeared mentally ill, diagnosis was often a challenge. In 1909, however, Drs Redington and Dwyer outlined a case of the newly described 'maniacal-depressive insanity' (bipolar affective disorder), with a good outcome, although the patient's history involved multiple episodes of disturbance, repeated admissions to the Richmond, and very little by way of specific treatment, apart from asylum admission.[11] Nonetheless, Redington and Dwyer's patient enjoyed sustained periods of wellness, and appeared to be a clear-cut case of the newly described disorder.

Other patients' symptoms were more obscure and less remitting. Maurice L., a 48-year-old single medical doctor, was admitted to Grangegorman from Hartfield House, a private asylum in Drumcondra, Dublin in the early years of the twentieth century. Maurice's half-brother was the formally appointed 'guardian of the lunatic' and provided much-needed background information:

> The patient is an unmarried man. When he was qualified about 25 or 27 years ago, he went to sea as a medical doctor on passenger steamers plying between Australia and Great Britain. He was at this for a few years, came back and settled down... I believe he drank consistently for the last 10 or 12 years and his constitution must have been very good to have withstood the effects of it. [Two years ago] he began taking morphia and this, together with his previous mode of life, has been the cause of his mind giving way.

On admission, Maurice was 'depressed and rather nervous', 'pulling at his moustache and fidgeting'. He said that 'he would like to die as he knows nothing'. Maurice told the asylum doctor that he started taking morphine three and half years earlier, for sleeplessness, and was now addicted to it. A week after admission, Maurice said that he was 'supposed to be a doctor' but claimed that he never qualified in medicine:

> I want to tell you an absolute fact, doctor. I hope you don't consider it a delusion. I am not a doctor at all. I never studied medicine... I had the name of being a doctor. I never had any trade or profession and I never earned a farthing in my lifetime. I was born a freak without brains... I am doomed to live this unfortunate life of mine forever.

A month after admission, the asylum doctor recorded that Maurice did not know the day or date, and 'says he is perfectly indifferent to his fate'. Two months later, Maurice was 'very depressed' and 'noisy day and night, cursing and blaspheming. Says he is doomed to live forever as a criminal and a lunatic'.

Maurice clearly presented a diagnostic puzzle to the doctors. As well as abusing alcohol and morphine, he was plainly depressed and seemingly psychotic, having lost touch with reality in several important respects. But whatever his diagnosis, Maurice's suffering was never in doubt. He talked constantly: 'Oh, if I only could get out of here— the curse of Jesus on you all'. He wished he was dead. He said 'there was never anybody like him', claiming that he was 'not like a man or a woman or an angel or a devil or an ape. He is like nothing. He was always so—was never natural'.

In this profoundly disturbed state, Maurice was transferred to the Portrane branch asylum after five months in the Richmond. There is no further record of his progress there, apart from the fact that he died in Portrane in 1920, possibly tormented to the end.

There were many similar cases of persistently symptomatic mental illness at the Richmond and Portrane, including cases of 'catatonic stupor', possibly the most life-threatening condition of all. Catatonia is now rare in areas with access to modern anti-psychotic medication, but it was relatively common in the asylums of the nineteenth and early twentieth centuries. 'Catatonic stupor' occurs when severe, untreated psychiatric symptoms are mirrored in the body. The patient's muscles are affected in such a way that they engage in unusual movements or sustain difficult, sometimes symbolic postures for impossibly long periods of time. Conolly Norman reported some such cases in vivid detail in 1905:

> Katatonic stupor passes on into, or is connected with, or is subdivided into, the ecstatic form. The girl who sat on the third chair rolled her eyes as if she saw visions. [Another patient] lay on her back with her arms stretched out rigidly—I think in imitation of the Crucifixion—and rolled her eyes about as if she saw visions. This condition ended in a true epileptic fit. She has had a number of epileptic fits and a number of these ecstatic

conditions...and sometimes (if I am right) she is blind.[12]

Quite apart from these severe forms of mental and physical illness, like catatonia, asylums were also dangerous, brutal places where accidents and injuries were common and patients occasionally killed each other—and themselves. Norman highlighted one such case at the Richmond:

> A patient in this asylum some years ago murdered another patient. He was sent to another asylum and slept in an associative dormitory, and there he smashed in the head of another patient with the chamber utensil. He was then placed in a single room—and hanged himself.[13]

Notwithstanding these clear problems, the asylums continued to accept large numbers of admissions in the early decades of the twentieth century. As usual, some of those admitted were demonstrably mentally ill, some intellectually disabled, some physically ill, and some just destitute and unwanted. The overcrowding dominated the Conference of the Irish Asylums Committee at Grangegorman in 1903, and caused Grangegorman itself to hold a special enquiry 'into the question of provision for workhouse lunatics', along with a diagnostic 'segregation' of its patients in 1907.[14]

Over the following decades, however, and during Ireland's revolutionary years (1912–1923), the asylums did not change: they simply adapted to the altered social and political circumstances in which they found themselves

(Chapter 8). In 1927 the Irish Free State published the detailed 'Report of the Commission on the Relief of the Sick and Destitute Poor, Including the Insane Poor', to try to address the issue.[15] But while there was no shortage of public, professional and political attention to the asylums, and certainly no paucity of official enquiries, no one had any solutions.

Despite the endless and arguably obscene succession of government reports, the numbers in the asylums continued grimly to rise. In 1929 Daniel L. Kelly, Inspector of Mental Hospitals, reported with palpable alarm that 'the number of insane persons under care on the 31st December, 1929, in public and private establishments, was 20,050'.[16] Despite plentiful public rhetoric bemoaning the size and condition of the asylums, the institutions continued to grow well into the middle of the twentieth century. And it was asylum staff who were left to manage the intractable, disquieting consequences of society's insatiable hunger for institutionalising the mentally ill.

## Chapter six

# "Dealing with the nervous system."

# 'No branches of medicine, anatomy, and physiology attract more attention or better workers at present than those dealing with the nervous system.'

Dr Conolly Norman, RMS, Richmond District Asylum (1894)[1]

The Richmond had a large complement of staff with a clear hierarchy that was evident at all times and in all aspects of the asylum's operations. The establishment was run by the lay 'moral manager' until the middle of the nineteenth century, at which point senior medical figures took charge and proceeded to exercise extraordinary power over patients and staff alike.

As the leading asylum of the day, the Richmond set the tone for district asylums across the country in relation to staffing. In 1848, following the death of Dr Alexander Jackson, Dr John Mollan became senior physician at the Richmond and placed an especially strong emphasis on moral management, the asylum school and library, and occupation as therapy. These priorities were quickly echoed throughout the rest of the Irish asylum system.

Mollan was succeeded by Dr Joseph Lalor who served as RMS from 1857 to 1886, and paid particular attention to the Richmond school, considering education to be the fundamental basis of moral treatment of the insane.[2] Lalor's successor, Dr Conolly Norman, brought the asylum into the 1900s, serving as RMS from 1886 until his death in 1908. Norman was energetic, progressive and deeply committed to reform, but he struggled with many problems at the Richmond, including overcrowding, beri beri, rampant tuberculosis and the inappropriate admission of people with intellectual disability, which troubled him deeply.[3]

Staffing was one of the key challenges faced by Norman and the other RMSs. Initially, Irish asylum attendants tended to come from rural areas and one of their key roles was to impart skills to patients to assist them in finding employment or contributing to the upkeep of the asylum (e.g. working on the asylum farm). Life was generally difficult for attendants and they were poorly paid, receiving significantly less than asylum attendants in England or farm labourers in Ireland.[4] They worked long hours, their social standing was low, and, for many years, they did not receive significant training. The first set of lectures given to mental health nurses was delivered by Sir Alexander Morison at Surrey Asylum in 1843–44. The Medico Psychological Association (MPA) later introduced a handbook for 'attendants' in 1885, with examinations some years later. But, generally speaking, asylum staff were poorly trained, if trained at all, for most of the nineteenth century.

The staffing system at the Richmond was based on hierarchy and control, rather than expertise or skill. The 1903 'Regulations for the Management of the Richmond District Asylum' set out extensive responsibilities for the 'Head Nurse', stating that 'she shall reside in the asylum' and shall be 'subject to the authority of the RMS, to whom she is to report daily, stating any irregularity or misconduct that may occur'.[5] The regulations outlined the Head Nurse's duties in some detail, including the following tasks:

- 'She shall take care that cleanliness, both in person and dress, is strictly adhered to, and shall have particular regard to the rooms in which sick, refractory, or idiotic patients are confined.'
- 'She shall pay occasional unexpected night visits to see that the Night Nurses are at their posts.'
- 'She shall employ the female patients as advantageously as possible to themselves and to the establishment, and in every way endeavour to promote their comfort and well-being.'
- 'She shall pay strict attention to the state of the laundry, and to the order and regularity in which it is conducted, and take care that the clothing, bedding, and linen of the patients, officers, attendants, and servants are properly washed, dried, aired and duly distributed, and the patients' clothing kept in a good state of repair.'
- 'She shall be present during the meals of the female patients, and promote habits of regularity, decorum, and cleanliness among the patients, and due attention on the part of the nurses.'

The RMS exercised considerable control over the staff, including the Head Nurse, who, like the others, could 'not be absent from the asylum without the sanction of the RMS'. The 'Head Attendant' had duties similar to those of the 'Head Nurse' but for male patients. The genders were kept strictly separate:

> No male attendant shall enter the female departments, nor female attendant enter the male departments, without the sanction of the RMS, or, in his absence, of the Assistant Medical Officer.

The 'Head Attendant' had responsibility to 'supervise the management of the male wards, maintain discipline and exercise supervision over the attendants and male patients, subject to the control and direction of the RMS. He shall instruct the attendants of the respective disciplines in their duties, and require their observance of all the regulations and orders'.

The 1903 Regulations also required that 'every attendant or nurse must undergo a period of training in the care and management of the sick and insane'. The attendant or nurse had to obtain the MPA's Certificate of Proficiency in Mental Nursing or else lose their post. This was an important regulation, given the tendency for asylums to engage unqualified staff. As late as 1951, Dr Joseph Kearney, Inspector of Mental Hospitals, reported that half of the staff at Kilkenny Mental Hospital did not have any nursing qualifications.[6]

Back in the Richmond in 1903, 'attendants and servants' were 'directly responsible to the RMS, and shall observe habits of cleanliness, order and subordination'. Staff lived on site, could not receive visitors without permission, and were obliged to be kind to patients or else face 'instant dismissal':

> Any attendant ill-treating a patient shall be liable to instant dismissal, and to prosecution,

and any attendant witnessing the ill-treatment of a patient by another attendant without reporting it shall be liable to a like penalty. Attendants are to avoid any harsh or intemperate language to patients, and must, by steadiness, kindness, and gentleness endeavour to contribute to that system of moral government upon which the value of the asylum depends.

These were the rather stern regulations governing staff at the Richmond in 1903, as the opening decades of the twentieth century brought considerable change to both Ireland and the Richmond. The death of Dr Conolly Norman in 1908 marked the end of the long nineteenth century, which saw the Irish asylums emerge, grow, and transform into the unhealthy, unwieldy, unholy institutions that dotted the Irish landscape at the start of the 1900s. Much of the time, staff struggled to maintain order in the asylums, let alone deliver effective care.

Norman was succeeded by Dr John O'Conor Donelan, who served as RMS from 1908 until 1937. O'Conor Donelan was to oversee significant changes at the institution over this period as the Irish asylums were convulsed by industrial unrest among staff; the First World War presented new challenges to the Richmond (Chapter 7); Ireland's revolutionary years changed the political landscape forever (Chapter 8); and new 'physical treatments' for mental illness were introduced in the 1920s and 1930s, generally pioneered in Ireland at the Richmond (Chapter 9).

Before considering these developments, however, it is worth noting that, as these dramatic changes unfolded across the world, throughout Irish society, and in the Richmond, the core business of the asylum—admitting and discharging patients—continued apace. While a great many of these patients were poor, elderly and mentally or physically ill, others presented more idiosyncratic challenges that required a certain amount of flexibility on the part of the institution. The exceedingly strange case of Leon de Martaeleare is a good example of the random challenges faced at the asylum.

Leon, a Belgian by birth, was committed to the Richmond as a 'dangerous lunatic' in January 1914. Leon was a confectioner and restaurant proprietor who ran a tea-room at 125 St Stephen's Green in Dublin's city-centre. In early January, Leon and the manageress of his restaurant set out to drive to Castlebellingham, a village in county Louth, around 70 kilometres north of Dublin.[7] As Leon and his colleague passed through the village of Swords, a police constable stopped them and asked them, as a favour, to bring District Inspector Dowling to his home in nearby Balbriggan. Leon agreed. He further arranged that, on the return trip from Castlebellingham, they would collect the District Inspector from his home in Balbriggan and bring him back to Swords.

All was well until Leon arrived back in Balbriggan to collect the District Inspector on the way back to Swords, and he found that local police were waiting for him. Leon appears to have misunderstood and resented this and, en route to Mr Dowling's residence to collect him, Leon left his vehicle and fled to the seashore. The driver of the car and a police constable followed and found Leon lying on the sand. They returned him to the vehicle. Leon was in a state of great excitement at this point and, following an attempted examination by a doctor, Leon was committed to the Richmond.

Throughout his journey to the asylum and his admission thereafter, Leon repeatedly claimed that he had hidden £200 in gold (a very considerable sum of money) in the rocks at Balbriggan. This was regarded as a delusion until Leon eventually persuaded the Belgian consul and asylum attendants to bring him to the foreshore in Balbriggan, where they duly found £200 in gold coins hidden in a crevice. Following these adventures, Leon enjoyed a swift recovery and prompt discharge from the asylum.

Apart from the decidedly peculiar (and still largely unexplained) events of that day, Leon displayed no sign of mental illness whatsoever. Over the years following his discharge from the Richmond, Leon's business continued to prosper, albeit beset by various complexities. In January 1916, Leon was sued by an employee for alleged slander, as she said Leon publicly accused her of stealing money during the Christmas rush.[8] Later that year, following the Easter Rising in April, Leon made a claim to the Property Losses (Ireland) Committee, 1916 for £145, 10 shillings and six pence for stock and personal effects looted from his premises during the 'disturbances'. Payment of £84, 19 shillings and two pence was recommended by the Committee. None of these events presented the slightest indication that Leon was then, or ever had been, a 'dangerous lunatic'.

In May 1917, Leon was again summoned to court, along with his wife Kate, for allegedly using chocolate for the external covering of cake without the authority of the Food Controller, during the First World War.[9] Kate said they had the sugar in stock prior to the Food Controller's order. In any case, neither Leon nor Kate actually appeared in court because by the time the case came up, Leon had

been called up to the Belgian Army, Kate had gone with him to England, and the business had closed down. Leon's legal representative suggested to the judge that Leon was of more use in the Belgian Army than in court in Dublin, and the judge appeared to agree, imposing a nominal fine of just 10 shillings.

All told, Leon's story is just one of the many thousands of peculiar adventures that found their way to the Richmond over the years. Despite the undoubted strangeness of the episode, there is no real evidence that Leon was mentally ill. His subsequent career certainly demonstrates no sign of mental disorder. There is, however, clear evidence of the use of the Richmond and the idea of 'criminal lunacy' to resolve all kinds of awkward situations that cropped up, such as that presented by Leon in 1914. This practice continued at all of the Irish asylums well into the twentieth century—the use of the institutions to resolve social issues, community dilemmas and problems with law and order that had no real link with mental illness but for which no other solution could be found.

Consistent with this socially embedded position of the asylums, the opening decades of the twentieth century saw industrial relations became an ever more pressing issue in the institutions. In 1896, attendants at the Richmond attempted to form a union, the National Union of Asylum Attendants in Ireland, and while this was not recognised by the Board of Governors at the time, it was a clear statement of intent. The 1920s and 1930s were duly characterised by a series of seemingly interminable strikes across Ireland's district asylum system, as part of a broader wave of social change across Ireland and Europe over these decades.

The asylum strikes were driven by several factors, including low wages and poor working conditions in the large, unsanitary institutions. Assaults and injuries, such as burnings, were frequent and sometimes fatal. In 1918, attendants at Monaghan Asylum went on strike, demanding union recognition and improved pay, and they achieved moderate concessions from management as a result.[10] In early January 1919, however, the Monaghan dispute again intensified: staff occupied the asylum; the red flag was raised; and the 'Monaghan Asylum Soviet' was born. These dramatic moves secured improvements in both hours and pay for the workers, and set a rather decisive example for similar institutions, including the Richmond.

The position was especially complex in Ireland as opposed to England, because the early phases of Irish national autonomy led to various sacrifices as part of the progressive realisation of self-governance.[11] One of these trade-offs was timely improvement in conditions and training for asylum-workers. As a result, industrial action soon spread to asylums in Clonmel, Letterkenny, Ballinasloe, Cork and elsewhere, and various concessions were duly obtained.[12] At the Richmond, trade unionism became part of the fabric of the institution, with trade unionists like Luke Duffy (1890–1961), who was also a Labour Party politician, serving on the Committee of Management, and staff members like Mary ('Maura') Breslin (1914–84) keeping the spirit of the unions alive, even after the asylum strikes of the 1910s and 1920s finally ended.

The early years of the twentieth century saw many other changes at Grangegorman, in addition to the effects of industrial unrest. The First World War, in particular, brought substantial challenges to the institution.

## Chapter seven

# "Could it be mental telegraphy?"

# 'We all act according to our nature and not according to the dictates of reason.'

Dr Conolly Norman, RMS, Richmond District Asylum (1905)[1]

The First World War (1914–18) brought considerable change to Grangegorman. Over the course of the conflict, almost 9 million soldiers served in the British army, including 200,000 Irish soldiers. Up to 40,000 Irish soldiers died and many more received physical injuries or, as became apparent in the early years of the war, had to return home owing to mental troubles caused or worsened by the conflict.[2]

At the Richmond, a dedicated 32-bed unit was set up on the grounds of the main asylum in June 1916 to treat these men. The 'Richmond War Hospital' was part of a broader network of war hospitals established across Ireland and Great Britain for this purpose.[3] The return of so many wounded soldiers presented a real challenge, not least because medical officers at the front who usually identified *physically* wounded soldiers requiring treatment back home were increasingly coming across *psychological* or *psychiatric* cases and simply did not know how to proceed.

There was a veritable epidemic of 'shell shock' between July and December 1916, when some 16,000 cases were recorded in the British army alone, during the Battle of the Somme. Overall, 10 per cent of British casualties in the war had some form of shell shock or neurasthenia, a condition characterised by anxiety, fatigue, neuralgia, headache and depressed mood. Shell shock accounted for one seventh of all British army discharges. The condition partially overlapped with 'neurasthenia', so the terms 'shell shock' and 'neurasthenia' were sometimes used interchangeably in this population.

The term 'shell shock' gained particular currency following its use by Captain Charles S. Myers in the *Lancet* in February 1915.[4] The following year, again in the *Lancet*, Myers associated an especially broad variety of symptoms with shell shock, ranging from problems with memory, vision, smell and taste, to over-reaction and 'hyperaesthesia' (increased sensitivity in one or more body areas).[5] As a result of this medical attention, and the clear problems posed on the battlefield, the diagnosis of shell shock came into widespread use and a network of psychiatric facilities was established to assess and treat affected soldiers.

At the Richmond, the diagnosis of 'shock' first appeared in the main asylum record books in May 1916, following the Easter Rising of April 1916, the first armed action of the Irish revolutionary period. While admission rates at the Richmond fell during the Rising itself, the following weeks produced an interesting change in admission patterns. On 1 May, a woman was admitted with a diagnosis of 'recent melancholia due to shock' which, as Collins points out, may be the first time the word 'shock' appeared in the admission books of the Richmond.[6] The diagnosis of 'shock' was to appear some ten times at the Richmond in May 1916, the month immediately following the Easter Rising and immediately preceding the opening of the war hospital for soldiers affected by the First World War.

Some of the treatments initially proposed for shell shock at various war hospitals were notably disciplinary in nature, highlighting an apparent conflict between the private intentions of the soldier and a sense of public duty, leading to the use of isolation, restricted diet and even electric shocks to alter soldiers' behaviour. Other treatments were more psychological in tone, regarding war neurosis as attributable to unconscious psychological conflict in the soldier's mind. This approach led to treatments such as hypnosis and abreaction, which involved soldiers re-experiencing or re-living traumatic memories in an effort to purge them of their emotional impact.

There were, however, other, gentler approaches which certain authorities viewed as equally if not more effective, including treatments based primarily on rest and less intrusive forms of therapy, such as engaging in drama and music. There was also a clear need to provide treatment to soldiers who had pre-existing mental illnesses, such as depression, which were worsened by the war. Some soldiers had developed physical illnesses such as epilepsy or infectious diseases during the conflict, and these also required care.

Many of the war hospitals that dealt with physical and mental problems were located in psychiatric hospitals. Adapting psychiatric hospitals to their new roles was often complex, involving changes to physical infrastructure (such as installing x-ray machines), as well as intricate staffing rearrangements. Nevertheless, by 1919 there were, in England and Wales, 24 mental hospitals being used as war hospitals, 14 of which were for physically sick and wounded soldiers only; seven for nervous problems only; and three for both physical and mental problems. The Richmond War Hospital formed part of this broader effort in Ireland, along with Belfast War Hospital, Leopardstown Hospital in Dublin and the Hermitage Hospital in Lucan.

While the Richmond War Hospital was an administrative element within the larger Richmond asylum, the War Hospital was, in many important respects, separate from the main asylum.[7] In the first instance, a new and separate block was put at the disposal of the army for the War Hospital, and its patients did not appear on the main asylum's record books.[8] Also, the army agreed to pay 21 shillings a week per occupied bed—a rate that was distinctly advantageous for the Richmond's managers. The weekly cost per patient was under 14 shillings and the army provided clothing for its own patients, making the arrangement an especially lucrative one from the asylum's perspective.[9]

Between 16 June 1916 and 23 December 1919, the Richmond War Hospital treated 362 soldiers with shell shock and various other mental problems.[10] Outcomes were reportedly good: more than half of these soldiers 'were successfully treated and enabled to return to their homes without the blemish of having been certified insane', according to RMS Donelan.[11]

Gunner A is a good example of a soldier who did well in the Richmond War Hospital. Aged 38 years on admission, Gunner A was transferred from King George V Hospital, a 462-bed war hospital used for the treatment of physical injuries (now St Bricin's Hospital, Dublin). Gunner A arrived at the Richmond in a 'dull and somewhat depressed and worried' state. He complained of 'pain and bursting noises in his head and insomnia', according to medical notes:

He states that when he drops off to sleep he wakes up in a fright and fancies someone is about his bed. In his dreams he imagines he is running. He also complains much of perspiration over front part of his head and states that whenever he comes before a Military Board he loses control over himself. I notice he slurs some of his words and finds it very difficult to pronounce test expressions. He is in much worry about his wife and child. The child is ill and his wife cannot speak well.

Gunner A 'went to the Front' in 1916 and returned in April 1918, 'suffering from neurasthenia' and 'shell shock'. He 'had venereal (gonorrhoea) in Gibraltar when a young fellow. States he was caught in the middle of a field under shell fire in October 1917 but kept on and then broke down completely last April and was sent home'.

A week after admission, Gunner A was 'very much improved' and seemed 'to be getting more control over himself. He is not nervous when questioned. He states his head is less troublesome. He sleeps and eats well'. A week later, he was 'allowed out on pass every day for a walk. He is brighter and more cheerful and is far less nervous'. Gunner A remained 'much improved', 'very well conducted' and 'fairly rational in his conversation' throughout the rest of his time at the hospital, although he was still 'somewhat nervous under examination'. He was discharged after spending eight weeks in the War Hospital.

Gunner A's experiences were typical of the new establishment. Patients were not certified as insane, discharge was common and often prompt, and the therapeutic approach centred on rest, recuperation and gentle physical and mental activity. The Irish Automobile Club took soldiers out for drives while singers and dramatic groups, who had visited the main asylum in the past, visited more frequently and for longer periods. Sport and games featured strongly, as they did in the larger asylum.

Other, more specific treatments were provided for particular physical and mental problems in the Richmond War Hospital. Physical illnesses were especially challenging. The Irish asylums already had significant difficulties with physical illnesses, especially infectious diseases, in the decades leading up to the First World War. In 1915, the Inspectors of Lunatics expressed concern at the level of physical illness in the Richmond asylum generally:

> This institution continues to be maintained in excellent order. There was, however, as usual, a considerable number of casualties and of cases of zymotic disease [acute, infectious disease] during the year, the latter including dysentery [inflammation of the bowel], erysipelas [a skin infection], and enteric fever [associated with contaminated food or water]. A new sanitary block has been erected at the male exercise ground.[12]

These concerns persisted during the years when the Richmond War Hospital operated, as the main asylum recorded a 7.6 per cent annual death rate in 1917. There was a particular problem with tuberculosis,[13] which had become the single most common cause of death among asylum inpatients at this time.[14]

Malaria, too, was quite common in the War Hospital. In 1918, Private B was admitted, having previously been in Radcliffe War Hospital in Nottinghamshire. He had been in the service for four years in the Dardanelles, Salonica, Serbia, Macedonia and Egypt.

According to medical notes, Private B was 'thin', 'dull and mildly depressed' on admission. He seemed 'more or less despondent. He complains of some pain in his head and loss of memory. He states he used to hear some noise but this is now less troublesome and that he at one time thought he heard voices but these have also disappeared'.

Private B felt 'depressed at times and does not like to talk to anyone'. He 'had a slight touch of dysentery on his way home from Egypt and had malaria in Salonica', with some more attacks recently. In the week following admission, Private B had 'a slight attack of malaria', 'complained of some headache', and was treated with quinine (standard treatment for malaria). While his headache resolved, Private B remained 'dull and apathetic' and 'somewhat depressed'. Although 'much improved', he was still 'not quite as bright as one would wish', according to the doctor.

Three weeks later, Private B was 'quiet but rather distant in his manner. He is very 'feeble-minded' and is made a 'but' [sic] of by most of the more cheery patients. He tries to step dance [and] sing on invitation from his comrades. He has not the slightest idea of either. He is much improved in his physical appearance. Sleeps and eats well'.

One month later, Private B was 'bright and cheerful' although 'very feeble-minded' (i.e. possibly below average intelligence). One month later again, he 'was out on pass' (i.e. on leave from the hospital), 'took some drink', 'kicked up a row', and 'was brought back under escort'. Two uneventful months later, Private B was 'discharged to care of friends'.

Private B clearly had a range of problems, from malaria to possible 'feeble-mindedness' to misuse of alcohol, but was nonetheless discharged from the War Hospital after a few months, reportedly improved.

This was not uncommon: Private C had a similar set of problems and a similar outcome. Admitted in 1919, Private C was 'very pale and delicate looking; tongue, limbs and body tremulous'. Mentally, he was 'despondent and depressed. He complains of headache and dizziness and states he dreams a good deal about the Front. He complains of insomnia.'

Private C had joined the army in 1909 and 'served continuously since. Served in India where he got malaria for 3½ years before going to the Front in September 1914. Served in France till September 1916...He seems very much worn.'

One week after admission, Private C had 'improved considerably. He is brighter and more cheerful and states he is feeling very much better. His headache is less troublesome. He seems much happier and is allowed out for a walk every day. Sleeps and eats well.' After another week, Private C was 'very much improved mentally and physically' although he 'had one attack of malaria since his admission'.

A month after admission, Private C had 'improved very much both physically and mentally. He has become much stouter [regarded as a sign of recovery] and his pallor has disappeared. He is brighter and more cheerful in conversation. He sleeps and eats well'. Five weeks later, Private C was 'discharged, recovered, to his home'.

Physical treatments for mental problems at the War Hospital were outlined by a Dr Forde at the 1917 spring meeting of the Irish Division of the Medico Psychological Association.[15] Treatments included hot and cold baths (which reportedly helped restore the power of speech in some cases), Fletcher's syrup of the hydrobromates (a widely-used remedy for many ailments which often hastened recovery, according to Forde) and citrate of caffeine (the soldiers' favourite). Forde also used antipyrine, a non-steroidal anti-inflammatory medication like aspirin which alleviated pain, reduced temperature and helped with sleep, as is demonstrated by the case of Private D.

Private D was a single, 21-year-old Church of England private who was admitted in 1919, having been in the service for three and a half years. On admission to the War Hospital, Private D's tongue was 'tremulous' and his 'left arm somewhat disabled', according to medical notes. Mentally, Private D was 'dull, depressed, sullen and morose'.

Private D complained of 'pain and dizziness in his head and has hallucinations of hearing. He states he hears voices speaking in German to him at night and the past comes back to him in dreams. He also complains of insomnia. There is a red mark around his neck where I am informed he attempted to strangle himself with a boot-lace. He tells me he has no remembrance of this.

'He states he joined the army in March 1916 and went to the Western Front in July 1916'. He 'came back with pneumonia in November 1916 and went out again in January 1917.' He 'was taken prisoner in May 1917 [and] liberated last Christmas' (1918). Private D then 'got two months' leave', was called back in February 1919, and 'has been serving since...He says he was badly treated while in Germany and was employed carrying shells to the German lines.' He 'was wounded at the time he was taken prisoner'.

On his first night in the War Hospital, Private D 'complained much of headache in the early part of the night, got some antipyrine and slept after a time'. A week after admission, he was 'somewhat brighter and more cheerful when spoken to but is reserved and distant as a rule. He tells me he is now sorry for what he did and that he is feeling better. He is, however, of low grade intelligence. Sleeps and eats well'.

Not all patients could be managed successfully in the relatively relaxed environment of the War Hospital, and some had to be sent to the main asylum observation unit ('obs ward') for periods of time. Private E, also admitted in 1919, had been in service for 17 months when he presented to the War Hospital as 'nervous and tremulous', and 'irritable'. Mentally, he was 'depressed and hypochondriacal and complains of pain in his head and loss of memory and of noises in his head like that of the engine of an aeroplane. He also complains of bad dreams about the war and of insomnia, and states he feels nervous and frightened'.

Private E 'joined the army first in 1915 and was discharged as under age'. He rejoined in 1917 and went to the Front the following year, only to 'come home wounded in the left thigh' six months later.

Ten days after admission to the War Hospital, Private E was 'quiet and well conducted. He is, however, still hypochondriacal and seems depressed. He states he is feeling better. Sleeps and eats well.' Two weeks after admission, Private E became more 'restless and depressed':

A couple of days ago this man became very restless and depressed and was inclined to wander away by himself and would not keep on his recreation grounds. He had to be sent to the obs ward. He was, however, calmer next morning and shows signs of improvement. He is somewhat brighter and more cheerful but is still inclined to imagine he is worse than he really is. Sleeps and eats well.

A week later, Private E had 'become much stouter. He is improving slowly. He joins in games occasionally. He is still inclined to be dull and complains of headache occasionally but seems improved. The noises have disappeared. Sleeps and eats well'.

Most but not all patients recovered at the War Hospital, and some stayed on in the main asylum after the War Hospital closed on 23 December 1919. Others were transferred to Belfast War Hospital and a small number returned directly to active military service. William R. Dawson, Inspector of Lunatic Asylums in Ireland, president of the Medico Psychological Association (1911) and specialist in nerve disease for the British army in Ireland, provided statistics about outcomes in a 1925 paper in the *Journal of Mental Science.*[16]

Dawson noted that, of the 362 patients treated at the Richmond War Hospital, two-thirds were discharged to their friends or to ordinary military hospitals, two returned to duty (0.6 per cent), and 31 were sent directly to civil asylums. This was comparable with outcomes at Belfast War Hospital where, of 1,215 admissions received over 30 months, just 18 (1.5 per cent) returned directly to military duty. Outcomes were similar at other war hospitals.

Despite the low rate of return to military duty, the fact remains that majorities of patients in both the Richmond and Belfast War Hospitals were discharged to families and friends within months of admission. This marked a significant change from Ireland's general asylums, including the Richmond, where length of stay was commonly longer.

Private F, for example, a 24-year-old Roman Catholic private, was admitted to the Richmond War Hospital from Connaught Hospital, Aldershot in 1919. He had been in service for three years and had recently suffered from pneumonia. According to medical notes, Private F was 'bright and cheerful in his manner. He states he hears voices speaking to him. Sometimes they speak against him, sometimes not. This occurs when he is speaking to other people. He states it can hardly be imagination and asks: "Could it be mental telegraphy?" "It is not so bad lately." "I take no notice of them." "I pass them by".'

One week after admission, Private F was 'very well conducted', 'bright and cheerful. He seems to be losing his hallucinations. He states they don't trouble him much at present. He is looking very well. Sleeps and eats well.'

One week later, still 'bright and cheerful', Private F stated that 'he does not now hear voices and that it must have been all his own imagination. He sleeps and eats well'. The following week, Private F seemed 'rational at present. He smiles when asked about the voices and states he does not now hear them'. Three weeks later, Private F was 'discharged, care of father'.

Overall, the Richmond War Hospital differed significantly from the main Richmond asylum because it assumed a more progressive approach to treatment and recovery, especially with regard to enhanced therapeutic and recreational provision for patients, and early discharge. The patient profile was also different in the War

Hospital, because the soldiers were less troubled by social disadvantage and chronic physical ill-health than patients in the main asylum, and therefore had a better prognosis from the start.

Perhaps most importantly, the Richmond War Hospital pointed towards future innovations in admission procedures and the legal status of asylum patients. As RMS Donelan pointed out at the time, a majority of the Richmond War Hospital's patients were apparently restored to good mental health without ever being certified insane. This held lessons for Ireland's asylum system more generally, eventually resulting in the Mental Treatment Act 1945, which cemented the concept of 'voluntary patients' in Ireland: not every asylum patient needed to be detained.

The closure of the War Hospital in December 1919 brought to an end a short but fascinating passage in the colourful history of the Richmond. It also heralded the start of another distinctive phase in the institution's history, characterised by the increased politicisation of the asylum during the remainder of Ireland's revolutionary years, into the tumultuous 1920s.

## Chapter eight

# "Unsuitable for their purpose in almost every respect"

# 'Insanity is a disease unlike others. It has numerous social relations.'

Dr Conolly Norman, RMS, Richmond District Asylum (1905)[1]

The Irish asylums, including the Richmond, were primarily social rather than medical creations. As a result, they became intensely political at the start of the twentieth century, to the point of taking a stand against 'the British Government in Ireland' and even hiding fugitives during the 1920s.

The asylums closely mirrored the needs of communities and societies that sought custodial ways to deal with the mentally ill, the intellectually disabled and various others who did not fit in. Initially, the Richmond was run by moral managers rather than doctors, and a medical certificate was not required for admission. As was the case elsewhere, however, as soon as asylum beds were opened, they were immediately filled. Even when clinical professionals began to run the establishment in the 1850s and committal laws were repeatedly revised, admission numbers continued to rise.

There were powerful social, economic and political vested interests in keeping the Irish asylums open, busy and large. Socially, the asylums offered a ready, flexible method for dispatching family members or relatives: initial committal was easy, discharge was relatively common (e.g.

if a family member was needed at home or on the farm), and re-admission was not difficult (when they were no longer required). Economically, the asylums were enormous employers for local towns and uniquely powerful purchasers of goods and services from surrounding communities. The building contracts alone were monumental. Any local representative who suggested closing or even scaling down such an institution would face considerable opposition if not outright derision.

The Local Government (Ireland) Act, 1898 brought significant change to the administration of the asylums, including the Richmond.[2] The legislation established county councils, urban district councils and rural district councils. Each council became responsible for nominating a committee to run the local asylum, in place of the old board of governors. The last meeting of the Board of Governors of the Richmond District Asylum occurred on 11 May 1898 and the first meeting of the new 'Joint Committee of the Richmond District Asylum' took place on 25 May. The Joint Committee had 46 members, comprising 26 members representing Dublin city, 11 representing Dublin county, five representing Louth and four representing Wicklow. Nine had been members of the old Board.

The joint committee set up four sub-committees: supplies, visiting, works and building, and finance. The 'Visiting Committee', which comprised approximately half of those on the Joint Committee, was responsible for the day-to-day running of the Richmond and Portrane asylums. Despite these extensive reforms, however, the change in governance did not produce dramatic change in the Richmond or elsewhere: the Committees were, in many ways, just as autocratic as the Boards had been; admissions continued to rise; and the asylums remained the powerful local economic forces that they had been for many decades.

As a result, the Irish asylums remained important political actors at local and regional levels well into the twentieth century. This is attributable not only to their embedded social roles and economic clout, but also the highly charged political atmosphere of the 1910s and 1920s. The Richmond, located so close to key sites in the Easter Rising of April 1916, became especially politicised as the 1920s commenced, particularly during the War of Independence (1919–21).

Dr Eleonora Fleury (1867–1960) was one of the key medical and political figures during this period at the Richmond and Portrane. Born in Manchester, Fleury studied medicine at the London School of Medicine for Women and the Royal Free Hospital. In 1890 she became the first female medical graduate of the Royal University of Ireland and was awarded a doctorate in medicine (MD with Gold Medal) in 1893.[3] Fleury worked at Homerton Fever Hospital in London before moving to the Richmond and Portrane.

Up to this time, the Medico Psychological Association accepted only men as members but in 1893 Dr Conolly Norman at the Richmond put forward Fleury's name for membership. Following some discussion, the Association's rules were changed in 1894 and Fleury duly became the first female psychiatrist in Ireland or Great Britain. For this and more, she deserves considerable acclaim.

In addition to her medical duties at the asylums, Fleury had deep involvement in the Irish republican movement, often using the Richmond and Portrane asylums to conceal and assist wounded fugitives. The asylums were perfect for this task: enormous, crowded and labyrinthine. Fleury also took fugitives into her home on the Richmond's grounds. One witness recalls that one such 'removal' of a wounded republican fugitive 'brought the patient from a house in Prussia Street area to the house of Dr Fleury in Richmond Asylum'.[4] Fleury provided both safety and medical care.

As a result of these activities at both the Richmond and Portrane, Fleury was arrested and imprisoned in 1923. She was, however, by no means alone in her political activism in the asylums. In Ballinasloe, Dr Ada English was another pioneering Irish psychiatrist who was deeply involved in Irish politics and medicine during the first half of the twentieth century. One of the first generation of female medical graduates in Ireland, English spent almost four decades (1904–42) working at Ballinasloe District Asylum, later St Brigid's Hospital, in county Galway.

English was an executive member of Cumann na mBan (a republican women's paramilitary organisation) and spent several months in Galway gaol in 1921, for possessing nationalist literature. While in gaol, Ada was elected as a Sinn Féin TD (Teachta Dála, member of the lower house of the Irish parliament) in the Second Dáil (1921–22) and she participated on the anti-Treaty side in the Civil War (1922–23).[5]

Like Fleury, English's strong nationalist outlook was apparent throughout all aspects of her life, including her work in Ballinasloe, where she supported the move to have the Galway Arms emblazoned in place of Queen Victoria on the buttons of the staff uniforms and promoted the use of Irish-manufactured products in the institution. English was a close friend of leading political figures including Joseph MacDonagh, Patrick Pearse, Arthur Griffith, Liam Mellows and Éamon de Valera.

Fortunately for English and Fleury, their political views were in close accord with those of the Committees of Management in the asylums where they worked. In Ballinasloe, the Asylum Committee passed the following resolution on 12 June 1916:

> That we the members of the Committee of Management of the Ballinasloe Asylum, representing both the counties of Galway and Roscommon, determinedly protest against the exclusion of any portion of Ulster from the scheme of national government now about to be established in this country, and we call upon Mr John Redmond and the Irish party to oppose anything that would bring about an accentuation of the religious bitterness that apparently exists between the north and the rest of Ireland. We are willing to concede anything in justice to the *bona-fide* fears of our northern fellow countrymen, but the division of Ireland we will not have.[6]

On 11 July 1921, the Ballinasloe Committee went further, resolving that 'henceforth no communication of any kind be forwarded to any department of the British Government in Ireland'. Sentiment was similar at the Richmond and various other asylums throughout the country, including those in Carlow and Clonmel.[7]

At the Richmond, the Committee established in July 1920 was especially republican in outlook. Once appointed, Committee members promptly pledged allegiance to Dáil Éireann, 'the legitimately elected and constituted government of the Irish Republic'.[8] In fact, Dáil Éireann had been established in January 1919 by Sinn Féin candidates who won a majority of votes in the election of December 1918 and refused to sit in Westminster.

Against this background, the Richmond was soon in deep financial crisis owing chiefly to the politicised nature of the Committee. In late 1920, the Committee's chairperson, Mrs Jennie Wyse Power (feminist, nationalist and a founder member of Sinn Féin), announced that the asylum had food for the patients for a day or two only, and families were publicly requested to provide financial support to keep their family-member in the asylum. W.J. Murphy, Chief Clerk at Grangegorman, placed a stern notice about likely discharges in the national press in September 1920:

> Owing to the withdrawal of State Grants-in-Aid to Municipal and County Authorities in Ireland, and the consequent reduction in payments to the Asylum Authorities, and also to the withdrawal of subsidies on flour, coal, sugar, etc., previously in force, a position of financial embarrassment has been created which the Joint Committee must take immediate steps to meet.
>
> In the circumstance, they are obliged to consider the discharge of all patients who, while not certified as sane, are considered to be neither dangerous to themselves nor the general community, unless arrangements can be made by their friends to contribute to the cost of their maintenance.

There are 3,281 patients in the Richmond and Portrane asylums...It costs at present 25s [shillings] per week (£65 per year) to keep a patient in the Richmond Asylum or 150 per cent over the pre-war figure, this figure covering medical and skilled nursing attendance and administration expenses.

The problem was fundamentally a political one. Mr William P. Corrigan, legal advisor to the Richmond Joint Committee, recounts the circumstances that led to the standoff between the Richmond and the British Local Government Board, with the resultant financial crisis:

Towards the end of 1920 the British Local Government Board had made demands on the Joint Committee of the Grangegorman Mental Hospital, then known as the Richmond and Portrane Asylum,[9] for their books for audit purposes, which the Joint Committee refused having previously sworn allegiance to Dáil Eireann. The Local Government Board then refused to grant aid. My firm acted as legal advisers to the Asylum Joint committee and having been consulted by the chairman (the late Mrs. Jennie Wyse Power) of the Committee regarding the raising of money on the deeds or the property of the Asylum. She stated that they had no money to feed the inmates for more than a day or two. I approached the Bank of Ireland for an advance on the security of the deeds and this was refused unless the consent of the Local Government Board was obtained.[10]

Corrigan consulted with an old acquaintance, Mr W.E. Wylie, K.C. (King's Counsel) who usually advised the Joint Committee, at his residence, pointing out that 'if the Committee could not raise the money without the consent of the Local Government Board, the Committee would have no alternative but to open the gates and release some 400 inmates. Mr Wylie stated: "This will be a nice town to live in with Black and Tans [Royal Irish Constabulary Special Reserve], I.R.A. [Irish Republican Army] and lunatics abroad".'

Notwithstanding these problems, the asylum not only survived this crisis (and numerous others), but continued grimly to expand, despite the social and political tumult surrounding it, despite the persistent industrial relations problems of the 1920s, and despite ever-increasing alarm at the number of inpatients. The institutions had taken on a life of their own.

The early 1920s brought significant administrative changes and a great deal of uncertainty to the Irish asylums, especially the Richmond. In 1923, a single Inspector of Lunatics was appointed, reporting to the Minister for Local Government.[11] In 1924, Peace Commissioners, rather than Justices of the Peace, became responsible for committals under the Criminal Lunatics (Ireland) Act, 1838. But most significantly, the Corporation of Dublin was abolished in 1924 and this created particular problems for the Richmond Joint Committee, which by now counted some 29 Dublin Corporation representatives among its 46 members. These 29 representatives were instructed to remain on the Committee for the moment, but they refused on the grounds that they no longer had a mandate from the now-defunct Corporation. The upshot of this and various other complexities was that the Joint Committee was suddenly reduced from 46 to eight members, all of whom came from Louth and Wicklow. More members were appointed in 1925, at which stage the asylum's name was changed to Grangegorman Mental Hospital.

All of these changes heralded a period of great uncertainty and unstable management in Grangegorman and the other asylums around Ireland. By the mid-1920s, the asylums were, as Edward Boyd Barrett, SJ (Society of Jesus) wrote in *Studies*, 'in a bad way. They are overcrowded. They are both understaffed and inefficiently staffed. Curable and incurable cases are herded together. There is practically no treatment. The percentage of cures remains at a very low figure. Public money is wasted. The asylums are unsuitable for their purpose in almost every respect':[12]

It is lamentable that public interest is cold and public co-operation non-existent in the fight against mental diseases. There should be strong public demand for immediate reform of the asylum system, and the complete segregation and scientific treatment of curable cases should be insisted upon. Suitable asylums should be built—healthy, bright, beautiful homes, where patients would be enticed by every art to renew their interests in things. Nerve clinics should be opened in every populous district, where advice and treatment should be available for ordinary cases of nerve trouble and incipient insanity.

Boyd Barrett was right to highlight the problems in the asylums of the 1920s and the need for out-patient care. He finished his essay with a dark, apocalyptic warning that— as was feared for much of the nineteenth century—the problem of mental illness was again on the rise:

> The prevalence of nerve trouble is much greater than is realised. Delusions, hysterical symptoms, obsessions, sex abnormalities, and neurasthenia abound on every side, entailing much suffering and much evil. For all this there is at present little or no treatment. Ignorance and indifference prevail, while the danger increases.

The lack of treatment in the asylums to which Boyd Barrett referred was soon addressed in the most dramatic fashion. The 1920s, '30s and '40s saw the introduction of multiple controversial biological treatments for mental illness, including malaria treatment, insulin coma, convulsive therapy and lobotomy, in a series of desperate efforts to empty the institutions. As ever, the Richmond led the way in Ireland.

## Chapter nine

"Foot of a hare, the right eye of a wolf"

# 'The pathology of insanity is at present in a very obscure condition.'

Dr Conolly Norman, RMS, Richmond District Asylum (1905)[1]

A limited understanding of the physical brain, high-lighted by RMS Norman, was just one of the many problems besetting Irish asylum doctors in the early twentieth century. There was general agreement that the asylums were too large and discharge too difficult. The numbers seeking admission kept rising and families were reluctant to take patients home. There was often good reason for this. Some asylum patients remained disturbed for many years and could not be managed at home. Some families were simply too poor. The increasingly panicked doctors reasoned that biology might offer a path forward: either better biological understandings of the brain acquired through post-mortems or better biological treatments to help manage insanity and discharge patients from the institutions.

Against this background, the opening decades of the twentieth century saw a succession of novel biological treatments introduced to the asylums. The first of these extraordinary efforts was malaria therapy, which was commenced at Grangegorman Mental Hospital (as the Richmond was called from 1925 onwards) in the mid-1920s, by Dr John Dunne, Assistant Medical Officer. This remarkable treatment was first described by Austrian physician Dr Julius Wagner-Jauregg (1857–1940) in 1917. It involved giving patients malaria in order to treat general paralysis of the insane (GPI), which was advanced syphilis that affected the brain, a common diagnosis in the asylums.

Dunne heard about the new treatment in Belfast in 1925 and the following year presented results for 25 long-stay patients with advanced GPI in Grangegorman.[2] All patients who developed fever following inoculation with malaria also developed low blood counts. Some became jaundiced. Two got pneumonia. Mental improvements occurred after quinine, the standard treatment for malaria, was administered to the patients. Eight patients out of the 25 improved greatly; seven improved slightly; five were unchanged; and five died (two from GPI, two from seizures, and one from pneumonia). Despite these distinctly mixed outcomes, Dunne saw real possibilities in the new treatment.

Dunne's enthusiasm was borne out over the following years. By 1929 the death rate from GPI at Grangegorman had fallen to 5 per year, having been around 35 per year prior to malarial therapy.[3] Julius Wagner-Jauregg, who developed the treatment, won a Nobel Prize for it in 1927.

Emboldened by the apparent success of malarial treatment, asylum doctors in Ireland and elsewhere quickly moved on to other equally unlikely-sounding approaches that sought to facilitate discharge from the ever-growing institutions.

Insulin therapy, introduced in Grangegorman in 1938, was developed in the early 1930s by Manfred Sakel (1900–57), an Austrian psychiatrist and neurophysiologist. It involved administering insulin to produce comas five or six mornings per week until such time as either 50 to 60 comas had been induced or a satisfactory therapeutic response was seen. The patient spent up to 15 minutes in a deep coma on each occasion. Some patients developed convulsions during the therapy. Comas were terminated by the administration of glucose intravenously or via a nasal tube. Patients invariably became obese during the course of the treatment and complications included permanent brain damage. Between two and five per cent died.

In 1950, Dunne published a relatively detailed analysis of insulin treatment in Grangegorman and reported that 405 out of 605 patients treated with insulin recovered.[4] Despite apparently good outcomes such as these, however, insulin therapy was not a success. It went into decline in the late 1950s and early 1960s owing to the emergence of safer and more effective treatments for schizophrenia (chiefly antipsychotic medication) and growing disillusionment with insulin therapy within the medical profession. In any case, yet more new therapies arrived in Grangegorman and shifted attention away from insulin coma. These included, most famously, lobotomy and convulsive therapy.

Frontal lobotomy or leucotomy involved surgery on the front part of the brain. It was developed in the 1930s by Dr António Egas Moniz (1874–1955), a Portuguese neurologist who shared a Nobel Prize for his work in 1949. Two types of lobotomy were developed. In a 'prefrontal lobotomy', the doctor drilled holes on the top or in the sides of the patient's skull to access the frontal lobes of the brain in order to sever connections between different parts of the front of the brain. In 'transorbital lobotomy', the doctor accessed the brain through the eye sockets to perform the same procedure. Transorbital lobotomies could be performed outside an operating room, took less than 10 minutes, and left no scars, apart from black eyes. A controversial treatment, lobotomy was said to reduce feelings of anxiety and introspection, as well as emotional tension and catatonia (severe mental disorder). In Ireland, lobotomy was introduced to Grangegorman patients in April 1946, with Mr Adams Andrew McConnell (1884–1972) performing the surgery at Richmond Surgical Hospital.[5] Several hundred lobotomies were performed.

Dunne reserved lobotomy for Grangegorman patients who had not improved with other treatments and still had severe symptoms. By mid-1947, 23 lobotomies had been performed. Three patients became well enough to be discharged home but others who were less disturbed following the surgery still had to be cared for within the hospital.[6]

In 1950 Dunne reported the outcomes of 63 Grangegorman patients with schizophrenia and poor prognosis who underwent lobotomy and found that 19 recovered sufficiently to be discharged; 19 had considerable improvements in behaviour; 18 showed no change; four disimproved markedly; and three died. With such mixed results, lobotomy went into decline during the 1950s and it remains one of the most tragic episodes in the history of psychiatry, a disturbing example of therapeutic enthusiasm that went unchecked for far too long.

The final and only lasting biological treatment from this era was convulsive therapy, based on the idea that epileptic seizures were therapeutic in people with mental illness. This treatment was introduced by Ladislas Joseph Meduna (1896–1964), a Hungarian neurologist, and further developed by Ugo Cerletti (1877–1963), an Italian neurologist, among others. Initially, seizures were induced using medication, especially Cardiazol, but electricity was later used, applied across the brain to produce the epileptic-type seizures ('convulsions' or 'fits') required for the treatment to work.

Cardiazol convulsive therapy was practiced throughout the Irish asylum system from 1939 onwards and in 1942 Dunne introduced ECT at Grangegorman. For the treatment, patients lay on their bed and electrodes were held against both temples. At first, during the 1940s and early 1950s, the small electric shock was generally administered without anaesthesia or muscle relaxants, with the result that the patient had a full seizure, usually for less than a minute. Afterwards, the patient felt groggy and likely had a headache. Before the introduction of anaesthesia, there was also a risk of physical injury from jerking movements during the seizure.

Many patients received this treatment a number of times per week, for several weeks. It was widely used for a range of conditions, especially depression. In 1950, Dunne reported that 209 out of 327 patients with 'involutional melancholia' (depression) 'recovered' following ECT.

The use of seizures to treat mental illness was somewhat ironic given the problems that epilepsy itself presented to the asylums, including Grangegorman. Dr Eveleen O'Brien, a medical officer in Grangegorman, devoted her 1939 doctoral thesis to 'Epilepsy and its Theories' and was clearly fully aware of the challenges presented by 'the epileptic seizure - with its sudden onset, its apparent absence of cause, its terrifying manifestations and its grim recurrences'.[7]

Despite long-standing recognition of the condition in medicine, history and literature, the cause of epilepsy

remained obscure. O'Brien outlined the known history of the condition in her thesis, theories about causes, and treatments offered in the past, ranging from the brutal (burning or cauterising veins in the head) to the bizarre:

> Amulets (especially those containing paeony root) were worn. Charms and spells of all kinds were invoked and many other prescriptions—pearls, castor, peacocks dung, foremost foot of a hare, the right eye of a wolf, the heart of a wolf, the liver of a young whelp [puppy], goosedung, corals, urine, were used.[8]

O'Brien took a grounded, pragmatic approach to epilepsy at Grangegorman, noting that treatment 'is still [in 1939] varied but it is not so bizarre. It resolves itself into two stages: (a) treatment during a seizure, and (b) treatment between the seizures.' O'Brien felt that 'the question of diet is of real importance', but focussed especially on various combinations of bromides (sedatives) and other medications. Careful, monitored treatment produced good results, she claimed:

> My experience in the treatment of epileptics has been a happy and encouraging one. The total number of fits for three months previous to treatment was 1,144 [...] The total number of fits for the same patients during the last three months on treatment was 128—a decrease in fit incidence for all cases of 88 per cent. The vast majority have improved—some to a remarkable extent [and] many epileptics are

grateful for one's poor efforts to improve their lot. [...] Work on their behalf is well advised. It will at some time lead to the cause and the cure. It will at all times make lighter the way of those 'that are lunatic and are sore vexed'.[9]

O'Brien was a remarkable figure who also worked with Dunne on insulin therapy.[10] Together they saw Grangegorman move through the era of new biological treatments in the early 1900s and into a quite different phase of its existence in the latter part of the century. In fact, by the time Dunne retired in 1965, Grangegorman had changed beyond all recognition.[11] Since his earliest days at the institution in the 1920s, Dunne had seen malaria therapy, insulin coma and lobotomy come and go. ECT was the only novel physical therapy to survive, along with O'Brien's renewed focus on the careful, measured treatment of epilepsy.

Over this time, Dunne not only introduced these new treatments to Grangegorman and (more importantly) studied their outcomes, but also made many pragmatic changes to the running of the institution: he reduced patient numbers, provided for better living and sleeping conditions, enhanced library facilities, appointed social workers, and made moves towards modern rehabilitation programmes.[12] Dunne was, in many ways, an essential bridge between the asylum-based past and the community-oriented future of psychiatry in Ireland.

Before moving on to the most recent phase in this history, however, it is worth pausing to note two things that do *not* feature in the history of the Irish asylums. First, and most remarkably, the Irish asylum system was one of the few networks of Irish institutions in which the Roman Catholic Church was not centrally involved. There were chaplains in the asylums and religious figures on the Boards of Governors, but the Church never took a central role in the provision or organisation of psychiatric care or running the asylums. Why not?

The answer lies in the fact that the asylums were, from the outset, linked with other government institutions, such as workhouses and prisons, rather than general medical hospitals, in which the Church was deeply involved.[13] In addition, the Church was arguably too busy for the asylums anyway, given its involvement with medical care, maternity care, schools, orphanages and laundries. There was also a sense that the mentally ill were not necessarily the 'deserving poor', and that other causes were more worthy of the Church's attention. Whatever the reason, the Church largely steered clear of the asylums.

The second notable non-event in the history of psychiatry in Ireland is the failure of Sigmund Freud or psychoanalysis to have a substantial impact on Irish psychiatry in the early twentieth century. Even in 1963, the Irish Psycho-Analytical Association had just five practising psychoanalyst members, and the movement never really caught hold in the Irish psychiatric community.[14] Again: why didn't it?

There are many reasons for this, including Ireland's peripheral location on the edge of Europe, Ireland's particular belief in institutionalisation as a solution to mental illness (and much else), and a distinct lack of interest in psychoanalysis among leading Irish psychiatrists. Even the old idea of 'moral management', which might reasonably have transformed itself into some form of psychological therapy, was not developed in this way. It led instead to a more traditional form of occupational therapy in the Irish mental hospitals.

At root, though, the key reason for the absence of psychoanalysis from Irish psychiatry likely lies in Irish psychiatry's traditional distrust of any form of ideology. While other countries experienced dramatic waves of psychoanalytic thought, revolutions in cognitive and behavioural psychology, 'anti-psychiatry' challenges to orthodox practice, and even—in Italy—an exotic alliance of left-wing ideology and radical psychiatric reform, Ireland experienced essentially none of these things. Irish psychiatry never had much interest in ideology and, arguably, still does not.

Instead, Ireland experienced an extremely slow *administrative* shift away from institutional care during the 1960s, '70s and '80s—a shift so gradual that is was almost imperceptible for much of the time. There were, however, definite incremental improvements to hospital conditions in the mid-twentieth century, such as those introduced by Dunne at Grangegorman, followed by some more visible steps forward, such as those made by Dr Dermot Walsh and Professor Ivor Browne, over the following decades.

These changes occurred not as a result of any ideological shift in Irish psychiatry, but as part of broader social change in Ireland during the 1970s and '80s. Finally, as Ireland itself modernised, the ground started to shift beneath Grangegorman. Very quietly, Ireland's seemingly inviolable network of mental hospitals slipped into terminal decline. After almost two centuries, the era of the asylum was coming to a gradual close with barely a whimper.

## Chapter ten

# "The peculiar mix of help and harm"

# 'Our best interests are identical with the interests of our patients and of the public, and are also the common interests of science.'

Dr Conolly Norman, RMS, Richmond District Asylum (1894)[1]

In 1915, Aidan K., a 68-year old married man, was admitted to the Richmond District Asylum from the 'Royal Hospital for Incurables' in Donnybrook, a Dublin hospital for the poor. The reason for admission to the asylum was 'cerebral haemorrhage'; i.e. bleeding in the brain that resulted in a stroke, seven years earlier. When he arrived at the Richmond, Aidan was a 'very feeble old man' with 'paralysis of the left arm and leg' from his stroke. He was 'unable to walk' because his right leg was 'contracted'; i.e. permanently shortened owing to spasticity of the muscle from another, earlier stroke.

In Grangegorman, Aidan was 'incoherent' and 'his speech [was] thick and very indistinct'. He had 'no idea of time'. A week after admission, Aidan became 'more feeble' and the following week he slipped into 'a stuperose condition'. A week later, Aidan died having spent less than three weeks in the asylum.

Essentially, Aidan was sent from a 'hospital for incurables' to an asylum to die, owing not to mental illness but to physical illness (repeated strokes). This was a recurring problem in the Irish asylums: not the admission of the mentally ill (although that was deeply problematic too), but the admission of society's unwanted, the physically sick, the poor, the dying, the destitute, the abandoned—those who did not fit in.

As we have seen, the decades following Aidan's death saw great activity and multiple therapeutic innovations at Grangegorman, including malaria therapy, insulin coma, lobotomy, ECT and various efforts to improve the experiences of patients and staff, and finally empty the mental hospitals. But despite these changes at the institution, Grangegorman remained precisely that: an institution. There was plenty of reformist zeal, but the experience of many patients in the twentieth century remained stubbornly similar to what it had been a century earlier: crowded, cramped conditions, poor diet, exposure to illness and injury in the asylum, and prolonged, if not life-long, institutionalisation.

Change was needed. In 1947, new legislation, the Mental Treatment Act 1945, heralded important (if belated) changes to Irish mental health law, including a new form of voluntary admission. While the new legislation failed to stem the rise in admissions, it set the scene for the single-most important step in de-institutionalisation in Ireland, the 1966 *Report of the Commission of Inquiry on Mental Illness.*[2] This influential Commission was appointed in 1961 by Seán MacEntee, Minister for Health, to report on services available to the mentally ill and propose improvements for the future. This it did, with gusto.

The '1966 Report' was published in 1967 and acknowledged mental illness as 'one of the major health problems of modern society'.[3] It highlighted Ireland's traditionally institutional approach to the mentally ill, pointing out that, 'in Ireland, approximately 7.3 psychiatric beds were provided in 1961 per 1,000 of the population; this rate appears to be the highest in the world and compared with 4.5 in Northern Ireland, 4.6 in England and Wales, 4.3 in Scotland, 2.1 in France and 4.3 in USA'.

Despite this distinctly dispiriting starting point, the Commission was hopeful that all of this could change:

> In the last few decades, psychiatric knowledge and methods have undergone a profound advance; and further progress no doubt lies in the not too distant future. There has been no similar period of time in the past which has seen such a marked improvement in therapeutic practice. The change has been due in part to the therapeutic possibilities opened up by the many pharmaceutical discoveries of recent times; but it has also come from a deeper understanding of the aetiology of mental ailments and of the needs of the mentally ill.[4]

The 'pharmaceutical discoveries' to which the Commission referred centred on the most recent biological enthusiasm in psychiatry: anti-psychotic medication. The prototypical anti-psychotic medication, chlorpromazine, was introduced in France in the 1950s and was soon followed by a number of other agents, in tablet and injected forms, which assisted with moves towards de-institutionalisation in many countries, including Ireland.

But the 1966 Commission recognised that much more than medication was needed. It proposed 'radical and widespread changes'[5] to the mental health system, shifting psychiatric services away from 'barrack-like buildings, characterised by large wards, gloomy corridors, stone stairways, inadequate heating, inadequate sanitary and bathing facilities, and poor furniture and furnishings'.[6] They might well have been describing Grangegorman.

Instead, the Commission recommended

> short-term residential units in, or in association with, general hospitals. Such units would require to be adequately staffed and equipped, to be associated with the community services of a particular area, to be ready to treat all types of mental illness requiring short-term in-patient care, and to work in close conjunction with the other psychiatric services and with the general hospital.[7]

The report emphasised treating mental illness in general practice and providing more outpatient care, building on the outpatient clinics already established in several parts of the country. In 1965, St Brendan's Hospital (as Grangegorman was known since 1958) provided outpatient care to populations of 718,332 people in Dublin and 58,473 in Wicklow through nine outpatient clinics in St Brendan's, Crumlin, Mercer's Hospital, Dun Laoghaire, Ballyfermot, St Loman's (Ballyowen), Finglas, Killester and Balbriggan.[8] In 1965, this network of clinics provided 17,381 outpatient appointments to 5,200 patients, making the St Brendan's clinics the largest psychiatry outpatient service in the country.

Further change was still needed, however, and reforming psychiatrists such as Dr Dermot Walsh[9] and Professor Ivor Browne[10] continued the traditions of Mollan, Lalor, Norman, O'Conor Donelan and Dunne by seeking to dismantle unnecessary inpatient care and replace it with community-based alternatives. Finally, inpatient numbers started to decline. In 1960 there were 1,677 patients in St Brendan's; by 1970 this had been reduced to 1,223; and by 1980 it stood at 942. Fewer patients were admitted; many inpatients moved to community residences; and a small but significant number of long-stay patients remained. At national level, numbers were falling too: in 1963 there were 19,801 psychiatry inpatients in Ireland; by 1970 this had fallen to 16,403; and by 1980 it was 13,342.[11]

Decanting patients from the institutions, including St Brendan's, continued steadily throughout the remainder of the 1980s, reportedly heralding a 'new psychiatry' based on community care rather than institutions.[12] By 1990 there were just 7,334 psychiatry inpatients in Ireland; in 2000 there were 4,230; and in 2014 the number stood at 2,228—the lowest in over a century.

This process was not without complexity or cost. The homeless mentally ill became increasingly apparent on the streets of Dublin and elsewhere, and there was growing recognition of the plight of the mentally ill in Irish prisons. Both of these problems—homelessness and imprisonment of the mentally ill—carried more than a distant echo of the pre-asylum era when the mentally ill commonly ended up as vagrants, were imprisoned for long periods, or died of exposure and neglect. In 1997, as St Brendan's continued to be dismantled, two women living in sheltered accommodation for outpatients of the hospital were brutally killed in their home, in the very shadow of the iconic mental hospital that they once knew so well.[13]

When St Brendan's finally closed its doors in 2013, leaving only the modern Phoenix Care Centre in its wake, there was a curious mixture of relief, nostalgia and sadness.[14] But it is important not to get misty-eyed about the asylums. Patients died there too, in great numbers, killed by other patients or, more commonly, by illnesses such as tuberculosis that were rampant in the unhygienic, overcrowded institutions—institutions that were fuelled by a fatal combination of bad laws, a society toxically obsessed with incarceration, and psychiatric hospitals that spiralled out of control.

While the demise of Grangegorman was both necessary and inevitable, it would be wrong to forget its history, or to forget the peculiar mix of help and harm, caring and abandonment that was reflected in all of Ireland's asylums throughout the nineteenth and twentieth centuries. In order to remember these institutions properly and well, and continuously re-evaluate their legacy, it is imperative that asylum archives are protected for the future and are open to historians today.[15]

Despite their complexities—or, more likely, because of them—the buried stories of the Irish asylum patients need to be unearthed and told. Staff, too, deserve a voice, as they sought to provide comfort and care in institutions that made both tasks difficult and sometimes impossible to achieve.

It is also important that mental hospital buildings are repurposed where feasible to serve social functions that reflect the altruistic intentions of their architects. The transformation of Grangegorman into TU Dublin is especially apt in light of the emphasis the hospital placed on its highly progressive school and its position as a world leader in hospital education throughout the nineteenth century.

The history of the mental hospitals as societal institutions is complex and important. It is a story of good intentions that often went awry, a story of what happens when society rejects large numbers of its own (labelling people as lunatics, idiots or simply unwanted), seeks to lock them away, and then frustrates all efforts to re-integrate them back into their communities.

Against this compelling, conflicted background, Grangegorman and the other mental hospitals offered true asylum to many people who were rejected by a desperately uncaring society, and to whom asylum staff commonly showed great kindness. But there was also systematic disempowerment of the mentally ill, deep alienation within the institutions, and grossly disproportionate deprivation of liberty. This had to change: while kindness is good, freedom is better.

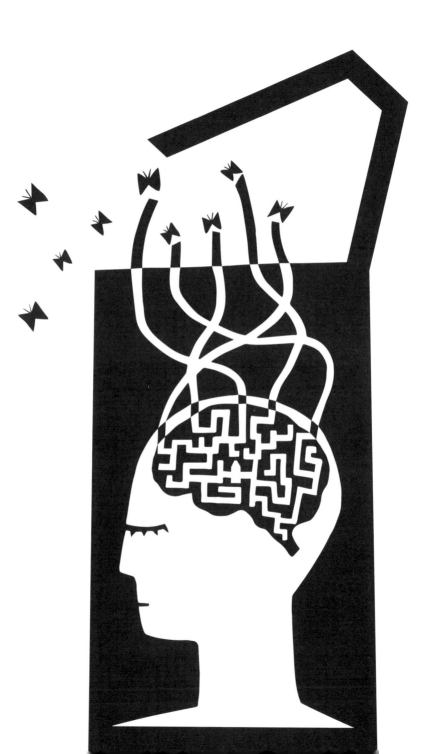

# Find out more about lives at Grangegorman

The Grangegorman archives are housed at the National Archives, Ireland under St Brendan's Hospital (PRIV/1223). To learn more, a good starting point is grangegormanhistories.ie, where you will see the work of the Grangegorman Histories project. The project provides a series of opportunities to contribute to the important work of uncovering, cataloguing and commemorating the eventful history of this site and the surrounding area. The website offers research aids, articles on the history and people of the site, and information on events and walking tours.

Grangegorman Histories is a public history project led by the Grangegorman Development Agency and the Royal Irish Academy with Dublin City Council, the Health Services Executive, the local communities, TU Dublin and the National Archives, Ireland.

# Endnotes

## Introduction

[1] Conolly Norman, *Conolly Norman lectures, Grangegorman* (Dublin: Royal College of Physicians of Ireland Heritage Centre, ACC/2017/2, 1905–7); Seventh Lecture, 20 March 1905 (CN/1/7, 2).

[2] Catherine Cox, *Negotiating insanity in the southeast of Ireland, 1820–1900* (Manchester and New York, 2012).

[3] Oonagh Walsh, 'A perfectly ordered establishment: Connaught District Lunatic Asylum (Ballinasloe)', in PM. Prior (ed.), *Asylums, mental health care and the Irish, 1800–2010* (Dublin and Portland, 2012), 246–70; Aidan Collins, *St Vincent's Hospital, Fairview: an illustrated history, 1857–2007* (Dublin, 2007).

[4] Damien Brennan, *Irish insanity, 1800–2000* (Abingdon, Oxon, 2014), 2.

[5] Joseph Reynolds, *Grangegorman: psychiatric care in Dublin since 1815* (Dublin, 1992); Brian O'Shea and Jane Falvey, 'A history of the Richmond Asylum (St Brendan's Hospital), Dublin', in Hugh Freeman and German E. Berrios (eds), *150 years of British psychiatry. Volume II: The aftermath* (London, 1996), 407–33.

[6] Brendan D. Kelly, *Hearing voices: the history of psychiatry in Ireland* (Dublin, 2016), 32–4.

[7] Brennan, *Irish insanity, 1800–2000*, 33.

[8] Select Committee on the Lunatic Poor in Ireland, *Report from the Select Committee on the Lunatic Poor in Ireland with Minutes of Evidence Taken Before the Committee and an Appendix* (London, 1817), 23.

[9] Joseph Robins, *Fools and mad: a history of the insane in Ireland* (Dublin, 1986), 26–39; Mark Finnane, *Insanity and the insane in post-famine Ireland* (London, 1981), 18–24.

[10] Elizabeth Malcolm, *Swift's hospital: a history of St Patrick's Hospital, Dublin, 1746–1989* (Dublin, 1989), 1–31.

[11] William S. Hallaran, *An Enquiry into the Causes Producing the Extraordinary Addition to the Number of Insane together with Extended Observations on the Cure of Insanity with Hints as to the Bet-

*ter Management of Public Asylums for Insane Persons* (hereafter *'An Enquiry'*) (Cork, 1810).

[12] William S. Hallaran, *Practical Observations on the Causes and Cures of Insanity (Second Edition)* (Cork, 1818).

[13] Brendan D. Kelly, 'Dr William Saunders Hallaran and psychiatric practice in nineteenth-century Ireland', *Irish Journal of Medical Science* 177 (1) (March 2008), 79–84.

[14] Thomas King Moylan, 'The District of Grangegorman (Part 1)', *Dublin Historical Record* 7 (1) (December 1944–February 1945), 1–15.

[15] Kelly, *Hearing voices*, 50.

[16] Select Committee on Lunatic Asylums (Ireland) (Advances) Bill. *Minutes of Evidence* (London, 1855).

[17] Dermot Walsh and Antoinette Daly, *Mental illness in Ireland 1750–2002: reflections on the rise and fall of institutional care* (Dublin, 2004), 17.

[18] Norman, *Conolly Norman Lectures, Grangegorman*; Nineteenth Lecture, 30 April 1906 (CN/2/18, 7).

## Chapter one

[1] Norman, *Conolly Norman Lectures, Grangegorman*; First Lecture, 3 March 1905 (CN/1/1, 1–2).

[2] Kelly, *Hearing voices*, 48.

[3] *Manchester Guardian*, 3 August 1833. Courtesy of Guardian News & Media Ltd.

[4] Cox, *Negotiating insanity in the southeast of Ireland, 1820–1900*, 76–7.

[5] T. Percy C. Kirkpatrick, *A note on the history of the care of the insane in Ireland up to the end of the nineteenth century* (Dublin, 1931), 30; Liam O'Brien, 'The magic wisp: a history of the mentally ill in Ireland', *Bulletin of the Menninger Clinic* 31 (2) (March 1967), 79–95; 88; Pauline M. Prior, *Madness and murder: gender, crime and mental disorder in nineteenth century Ireland* (Dublin and Portland, OR, 2008), 27–9.

[6] Reynolds, *Grangegorman: psychiatric care in Dublin since 1815*, 75–6.

[7] Finnane, *Insanity and the insane in post-Famine Ireland*, 100, 231.

[8] Reynolds, *Grangegorman: psychiatric care in Dublin since 1815*, 61–72; Robins, *Fools and mad: a history of the insane in Ireland*, 96–7, 135.

[9] John Mollan, 'Statistical report of the Richmond Lunatic Asylum', *Dublin Journal of Medical Science* 13 (3) (July 1838), 367–84.

[10] Alice Mauger, '"Confinement of the higher orders": the social role of private lunatic asylums in Ireland, c. 1820–60', *Journal of the History of Medicine and Allied Sciences* 67 (2) (April 2012), 281–317; Alice Mauger, *The cost of insanity in nineteenth-century Ireland: public, voluntary and private asylum care* (Cham, 2018), 2–8.

[11] Kelly, *Hearing voices*, 49.

[12] Inspectors of Lunatics (Ireland), *The Forty-Second Report (With Appendices) of the Inspectors of Lunatics (Ireland) 1892* (Dublin, 1893), 2.

[13] Norman R. Phillips, 'Daniel Frederick Rambaut', *Journal of Mental Science* 84 (348) (January 1938), 1–2. Rambaut went on to become Medical Superintendent at the County Mental Hospital in Shrewsbury (1902) and St Andrew's in Northampton (1913), as well as president of the Royal Medico Psychological Association (1934). See also: Aidan Collins, 'Daniel Frederick Rambaut: 'Rugbanian' and innovative resident medical superintendent', *Irish Journal of Psychological Medicine* 34 (1) (March 2017), 75–8. I am very grateful to Dr Aidan Collins for discussing this case with me.

[14] Richmond Asylum Joint Committee. *Richmond Asylum Joint Committee Minutes* (Dublin, 1907), 92–3.

[15] Brendan D. Kelly, 'One hundred years ago: the Richmond Asylum, Dublin in 1907', *Irish Journal of Psychological Medicine* 24 (3) (September 2007), 108–14.

[16] Brennan, *Irish insanity, 1800–2000*, 2.

## Chapter two

[1] Norman, *Conolly Norman Lectures, Grangegorman*; Thirty-Second Lecture, 30 May 1905 (CN/1/32, 11).

[2] Jean-Étienne Dominique Esquirol, *Des Passions* (Paris, 1805).

[3] Kelly, *Hearing voices*, 38.

[4] Hanora M. Henry, *Our Lady's Psychiatric Hospital Cork* (Cork, 1989), 528–35.

[5] Finnane, *Insanity and the insane in post-Famine Ireland*, 190–201; Cox, *Negotiating insanity in the southeast of Ireland, 1820–1900*, 207–12.

[6] Hallaran, *An Enquiry*, 46–7.

[7] John Mollan, 'Statistical report on the Richmond Lunatic Asylum', *Dublin Journal of Medical Science* 13 (3) (July 1838), 367–84; 379–80.

[8] Mollan went on to serve as president of the King and Queen's College of Physicians in Ireland (1855–6) and took an active part in the formation of the Royal Medical Benevolent Fund.

[9] Weeshie Fogarty, *Dr Eamonn O'Sullivan: a man before his time* (Dublin, 2007), 191–7.

[10] Eamonn N.M. O'Sullivan, *Textbook of occupational therapy with chief reference to psychological medicine* (London, 1955).

[11] Caren Prendiville and Judith Pettigrew, 'Leisure occupations in the Central Criminal Lunatic Asylum 1890–1920', *Irish Journal of Occupational Therapy* 43 (1) (Spring 2015), 12–9.

[12] Bríd D. Dunne, Katie Robinson and Judith Pettigrew, 'A case study of the development of occupational therapy at St Patrick's Hospital Dublin, 1935–1969', *Irish Journal of Occupational Therapy* 46 (1) (2018), 31–45.

[13] Brendan D. Kelly, *Ada English: patriot and psychiatrist* (Sallins, County Kildare, 2014), 54–9.

[14] Mental Treatment Regulations (Statutory Instrument 261 of 1961), Section 13.

## Chapter three

[1] Norman, *Conolly Norman Lectures, Grangegorman*; Thirty-Second Lecture, 30 May 1905 (CN/1/32, 13).

[2] Kelly, *Hearing voices*, 85, 121.

[3] Richmond District Asylum, *Regulations for the Management of the Richmond District Asylum under the Act 60 & 61 Victoriæ, Cap. 37* (Dublin, 1903) (National Library of Ireland, BB4120), 19.

[4] Richmond District Asylum, *Regulations for the Management of the Richmond District Asylum*, 20, 21.

[5] Richmond District Asylum, *Regulations for the Management of the Richmond District Asylum*, 20.

[6] John Mollan, 'Statistical report on the Richmond Lunatic Asylum', *Dublin Journal of Medical Science*, 13, 3 (July 1838), 367–84; 380.

[7] Tom Walsh, 'The national system of education, 1831–2000', in B. Walsh (ed.), *Essays in the history of Irish education* (London, 2016). 7–43. See also: Garret FitzGerald, *Irish primary education in the early nineteenth century: an analysis of the First and Second Reports of the Commissioners of Irish Education Inquiry, 1825–6* (Dublin, 2013).

[8] Joseph Lalor, 'On the use of education and training in the treatment of the insane in public lunatic asylums', *Journal of the Statistical and Social Inquiry of Ireland* 7 (54) (1878), 361–73.

[9] Daniel H. Tuke, 'On the Richmond Asylum schools', *Journal of Mental Science* 21 (95) (October 1875), 467–74; 468–9.

[10] Norman R. Phillips, 'Daniel Frederick Rambaut', *Journal of Mental Science* 84 (348) (January 1938), 1–2.

[11] Aidan Collins, 'Daniel Frederick Rambaut: 'Rugbanian' and innovative resident medical superintendent', *Irish Journal of Psychological Medicine* 34 (1) (March 2017), 75–8.

[12] Steven Cherry and Roger Munting, '"Exercise is the thing"? Sport and the asylum *c.* 1850–1950', *International Journal of the History of Sport* 22 (1) (2005), 42–58.

## Chapter four

[1] Norman, *Conolly Norman Lectures, Grangegorman*; Thirty-Second Lecture, 29 May 1906 (CN/2/31, 2).

[2] Norman, *Conolly Norman Lectures, Grangegorman*; Fifth Lecture, 13 March 1905 (CN/1/5, 6, 7).

[3] Niamh A. Kelly, *Imaging the Great Irish Famine: representing dispossession in visual culture* (London, 2018).

[4] Dermot Walsh, 'Did the Great Irish Famine increase schizophrenia?', *Irish Journal of Psychological Medicine* 29 (1) (January 2012), 7–15.

[5] Inspectors of Lunatics (Ireland), *The Sixty-Third Annual Report (With Appendices) of the Inspectors of Lunatics (Ireland), Being for the Year Ending 31st December 1913* (Dublin, 1914), xvi. See also: Melinda D. Grimsley-Smith, 'Politics, professionalisation, and poverty: lunatic asylums for the poor in Ireland, 1817–1920' (PhD thesis, University of Notre Dame, IN, 2011), 208–9; Cox, *Negotiating insanity in the southeast of Ireland, 1820–1900*, 38–9.

[6] Oonagh Walsh, 'An invisible but inescapable trauma': epigenetics and the Great Famine', in C. Kinealy, J. King and C. Reilly (eds), *Women and the Great Hunger* (Hamden, CT, 2016), 173–83.

[7] Brendan D. Kelly, 'The Great Irish Famine (1845–52) and the Irish asylum system: remembering, forgetting, and remembering again', *Irish Journal of Medical Science* 188 (3) (August 2019), 953–8.

[8] Richmond District Asylum, *Regulations for the Management of the Richmond District Asylum under the Act 60 & 61 Victoriæ, Cap. 37* (Dublin, 1903) (National Library of Ireland, BB4120), 20.

[9] Resident Medical Superintendent, *Richmond District Lunatic Asylum, Dublin: Report of the Resident Medical Superintendent for the Year 1862* (Dublin, 1863) (National Library of Ireland, Ir 3622 r1), 35.

[10] Bram Stoker, *Dracula* (London, 1897).

[11] Aidan Collins, 'Daniel Frederick Rambaut: 'Rugbanian' and innovative resident medical superintendent', *Irish Journal of Psychological Medicine* 34 (1) (March 2017), 75–8.

[12] Conolly Norman, 'The clinical features of beri-beri', *Transactions of the Royal Academy of Medicine in Ireland* 17 (1) (1 December 1899), 145–79.

[13] Conolly Norman, 'A brief note on beri-beri in asylums', *Journal of Mental Science* 45 (190) (July 1899), 503–12.

[14] E. Margaret Crawford, 'A mysterious malady in an Irish asylum: the Richmond epidemic of the late nineteenth century', in P.M. Prior (ed.), *Asylums, mental health care and the Irish, 1800–2010* (Dublin and Portland, OR, 2012), 185–204.

[15] Kelly, *Hearing voices*, 76.

[16] Grangegorman Mental Hospital, *'Vegetables Issued' Book* (Dublin Grangegorman Mental Hospital, 1916) (National Archives of Ireland, PRIV 1223/22/4).

[17] Norman, *Conolly Norman Lectures, Grangegorman*; Thirteenth Lecture, 3 April 1905 (CN/1/13, 10–11).

## Chapter five

[1] Norman, *Conolly Norman Lectures, Grangegorman*; Thirtieth Lecture, 26 May 1905 (CN/1/30, 1).

[2] Oonagh Walsh, 'Gender and insanity in nineteenth-century Ireland', in J. Andrews and A. Digby (eds), *Sex and seclusion, class and*

*custody: perspectives on gender and class in the history of British and Irish psychiatry* (Amsterdam, 2004), 69–93; 74–5.

[3] John Mollan, 'Statistical report on the Richmond Lunatic Asylum', *Dublin Journal of Medical Science* 13 (3) (July 1838), 367–84.

[4] Resident Medical Superintendent, *Richmond District Lunatic Asylum, Dublin: Report of the Resident Medical Superintendent for the Year 1862* (Dublin, 1863) (National Library of Ireland, Ir 3622 r1), 15.

[5] John Mollan, 'Statistical report on the Richmond Lunatic Asylum', *Dublin Journal of Medical Science* 13 (3) (July 1838), 367–84.

[6] Resident Medical Superintendent, *Richmond District Lunatic Asylum, Dublin: Report of the Resident Medical Superintendent for the Year 1862* (Dublin, 1863) (National Library of Ireland, Ir 3622 r1), 15.

[7] Kelly, *Hearing voices*, 76.

[8] English translation of the Latin phrase 'Homo proponit, sed Deus disponit', from *The imitation of Christ*, a 15th-century book by German cleric Thomas à Kempis (Book I, Chapter 19).

[9] Psalm 132/3 (Latin): 'Behold how good and how pleasant it is for brethren to dwell in unity'.

[10] 'Try to learn something about everything and everything about something'. This was a favourite comment of Thomas Henry Huxley (1825–95), a British biologist; it is inscribed on Huxley's memorial at Ealing and quoted in *Nature*, 30 October 1902 (Vol. XLVI, 658).

[11] J.M. Redington and P.J. Dwyer, 'Maniacal-depressive insanity amongst the male admissions to the Richmond District Asylum in the year 1907', *Journal of Mental Science* 55 (228) (January 1909), 56–8.

[12] Norman, *Conolly Norman Lectures, Grangegorman*; Thirteenth Lecture, 3 April 1905 (CN/1/13, 9–10).

[13] Norman, *Conolly Norman Lectures, Grangegorman*; Seventh Lecture, 20 March 1905 (CN/1/7, 12).

[14] Brendan D. Kelly, 'One hundred years ago: the Richmond Asylum, Dublin in 1907', *Irish Journal of Psychological Medicine* 24 (3) (September 2007), 108–14.

[15] Commission on the Relief of the Sick and Destitute Poor, Including the Insane Poor, *Report of the Commission on the Relief of the*

*Sick and Destitute Poor, Including the Insane Poor* (Dublin, 1927).
[16] Inspector of Mental Hospitals, *Annual Report of the Inspector of Mental Hospitals for the Year 1929* (Dublin, 1930), 5.

## Chapter six

[1] Conolly Norman, 'Presidential address, delivered at the Royal College of Physicians, Dublin, June 12th, 1894', *Journal of Mental Science* 40 (171) (October 1894), 487–99; 489.

[2] Anonymous, 'Obituary: Joseph Lalor, MD', *Journal of Mental Science* 32 (139) (October 1886), 462–3; Kelly, *Hearing Voices*, 44.

[3] Conolly Norman, 'Report of Dr Norman', in *Richmond Asylum Joint Committee Minutes* (Dublin: Richmond Asylum, 1907).

[4] Kelly, *Hearing voices*, 220.

[5] Richmond District Asylum, *Regulations for the Management of the Richmond District Asylum under the Act 60 & 61 Victoriæ, Cap. 37* (Dublin, 1903) (National Library of Ireland, BB4120), 37.

[6] Joseph Robins, *Nursing and midwifery in Ireland in the twentieth century* (Dublin, 2000), 36.

[7] Anonymous, 'Hidden gold: £200 found at Balbriggan', *Weekly Irish Times*, 31 January 1914.

8 Anonymous, 'Dublin slander action: Scully v De Martelaere', *Freeman's Journal*, 25 January 1916.

[9] Anonymous, 'Prosecution in the Dublin Police Court', *Evening Herald*, 16 May 1917; Anonymous, 'Irish news of the week', *Weekly Irish Times*, 26 May 1917.

[10] Anton McCabe and Ciaran Mulholland, 'The red flag over the asylum', in P.M. Prior (ed.), *Asylums, mental health care and the Irish, 1800–2010* (Dublin and Portland, Oregon, 2012), 23–43.

[11] Ann J. Sheridan, 'The impact of political transition on psychiatric nursing: a case study of twentieth-century Ireland', *Nursing Inquiry* 13 (4) (2006), 289–99.

[12] Kelly, *Hearing voices*, 165–6.

## Chapter seven

[1] Norman, *Conolly Norman Lectures,* Seventh Lecture, 20 March 1905 (CN/1/7, 2).

[2] Brendan D. Kelly, 'Shell shock in Ireland: the Richmond War Hospital, Dublin (1916–19)', *History of Psychiatry* 26 (1) (March 2015), 50–63.

[3] Ben Shephard, *A war of nerves: soldiers and psychiatrists, 1914–1994* (London, 2002), 73.

[4] Charles S. Myers, 'A contribution to the study of shell shock', *Lancet* 185 (4772) (13 February 1915), 316–20.

[5] Charles S. Myers, 'Contributions to the study of shell shock: being an account of certain disorders of cutaneous sensibility', *Lancet* 187 (4829) (18 March 1916), 608–13.

[6] Aidan Collins, 'The Richmond District Asylum and the 1916 Easter Rising', *Irish Journal of Psychological Medicine* 30 (4) (December 2013), 279–83.

[7] Brendan D. Kelly, *'He lost himself completely': shell shock and its treatment at Dublin's Richmond War Hospital, 1916–1919* (Dublin, 2014), 30.

[8] Aidan Collins, 'The Richmond District Asylum and the 1916 Easter Rising', *Irish Journal of Psychological Medicine* 30 (4) (December 2013), 279–83.

[9] Reynolds, *Grangegorman: Psychiatric Care in Dublin since 1815,* 217.

[10] Kelly, *'He lost himself completely'*, xiv.

[11] Reynolds, *Grangegorman: psychiatric care in Dublin since 1815*, 219.

[12] Inspectors of Lunatics (Ireland), *The Sixty-Fifth Annual Report (With Appendices) of the Inspectors of Lunatics (Ireland), Being for the Year Ending 31st December 1915* (Dublin, 1917), xxiv.

[13] Brendan D. Kelly, 'Tuberculosis in the nineteenth-century asylum: clinical cases from the Central Criminal Lunatic Asylum, Dundrum, Dublin', in P.M. Prior (ed.), *Asylums, mental health care and the Irish, 1800–2010* (Dublin and Portland, OR, 2012), 205–20.

[14] Inspectors of Lunatics (Ireland), *The Forty-Second Report (With Appendices) of the Inspectors of Lunatics (Ireland) 1892* (Dublin, 1893), 35.

[15] Anonymous, 'Irish Division', *Journal of Mental Science* 63 (261) (April 1917), 297–9.

[16] William R. Dawson, 'The work of the Belfast War Hospital (1917–1919)', *Journal of Mental Science* 71 (293) (April 1925), 219–24.

## Chapter eight

[1] Norman, *Conolly Norman Lectures, Grangegorman*; Thirtieth Lecture, 26 May 1905 (CN/1/30, 1).

[2] Reynolds, *Grangegorman: psychiatric care in Dublin since 1815*, 191–4.

[3] Aidan Collins, 'Eleonora Fleury captured', *British Journal of Psychiatry* 203 (1) (July 2013), 5; Aidan Collins, 'Fleury, Eleonora Lilian', in J. McGuire and J. Quinn (eds), *Dictionary of Irish biography* (Cambridge, 2014).

[4] Bureau of Military History 1913–21 Collection Witness Statements (Military Archives, Cathal Brugha Barracks, Dublin): *Witness Statement (Number 568) of Eilís Bean Uí Chonaill* (File Number S.1846), 54.

[5] Brendan D. Kelly, *Ada English: patriot and psychiatrist* (Sallins, County Kildare, 2014).

[6] Committee of Management of Ballinasloe District Lunatic Asylum/Mental Hospital, *Minutes of the Proceedings of the Committee of Management of Ballinasloe District Lunatic Asylum/Mental Hospital, 1904–1942* (Archives at St Brigid's Hospital, Ballinasloe, County Galway, Ireland).

[7] Kelly, *Hearing voices*, 154.

[8] Reynolds, *Grangegorman: psychiatric care in Dublin since 1815*, 224.

[9] The asylums' names were formally changed to Grangegorman Mental Hospital and Portrane Branch Mental Hospital by the Local Government Act, 1925 (Reynolds, *Grangegorman: psychiatric care in Dublin since 1815*, 225).

[10] Bureau of Military History. 1913-21 Collection Witness Statements (Military Archives, Cathal Brugha Barracks, Dublin): *Witness Statement (Number 250) of Mr William P. Corrigan* (File Number S.378), 1. See also: Kelly, *Hearing voices*, 150-4.

[11] Reynolds, *Grangegorman: psychiatric care in Dublin since 1815*, 227.

[12] E. Boyd Barrett, 'Modern psycho-therapy and our asylums', *Studies* 13 (49) (March 1924), 29–43.

## Chapter nine

[1] Norman, *Conolly Norman Lectures, Grangegorman*; Thirteenth Lecture, 3 April 1905 (CN/1/13, 9).

[2] John Dunne, 'The malarial treatment of general paralysis', *Journal of Mental Science* 72 (298) (July 1926), 343–46.

[3] Reynolds, *Grangegorman: psychiatric care in Dublin since 1815*, 239.

[4] John Dunne, 'Survey of modern physical methods of treatment for mental illness carried out in Grangegorman Mental Hospital', *Journal of the Medical Association of Eire* 27 (157) (July 1950), 4–9.

[5] Kelly, *Hearing voices*, 176.

[6] Reynolds, *Grangegorman: psychiatric care in Dublin since 1815*, 265.

[7] Eveleen O'Brien, 'Epilepsy and its theories: results of treatment' (MD Thesis, University College Dublin, 1939), 1.

[8] O'Brien, 'Epilepsy and its theories', 30.

[9] O'Brien, 'Epilepsy and its theories', 76.

[10] John Dunne and Eveleen O'Brien, 'Insulin therapy: a short review of the work done in Grangegorman Mental Hospital', *Journal of Mental Science* 85 (356) (May 1939), 498–504; Aoife K. O'Callaghan and Brendan D. Kelly, 'Dr Eveleen O'Brien (1901–1981)', *Irish Journal of Medical Science* 188 (2) (2019 ) 649–52.

[11] Liam MacGabhann, 'Dr Dunne retires after 45 years in St Brendan's', *Irish Times*, 31 December 1965.

[12] Kelly, *Hearing voices*, 169.

[13] Brendan D. Kelly, 'Ego, id and Ireland', *Lancet Psychiatry* 4 (4) (April 2017), 281–2.

[14] Kelly, *Hearing voices*, 170.

## Chapter ten

[1] Conolly Norman, 'Presidential address, delivered at the Royal College of Physicians, Dublin, June 12th, 1894', *Journal of Mental Science* 40 (171) (October 1894), 487–99; 489.

[2] Commission of Inquiry on Mental Illness, *Report of the Commission of Inquiry on Mental Illness* (Dublin: The Stationery Office, 1967).

[3] Commission of Inquiry on Mental Illness, *Report*, xiii.

[4] Commission of Inquiry on Mental Illness, *Report*, xiv.

[5] Commission of Inquiry on Mental Illness, *Report*, xv.

[6] Commission of Inquiry on Mental Illness, *Report,* 50.

[7] Commission of Inquiry on Mental Illness, Report, xv.

[8] Commission of Inquiry on Mental Illness, Report, 165.

[9] Brendan D. Kelly, 'Dr Dermot Walsh, 1931–2017', *Irish Journal of Psychological Medicine* 34 (3) (September 2017), 217–20.

[10] Ivor Browne, *Music and madness* (Cork, 2008).

[11] Antoinette Daly and Sarah Craig, *Irish psychiatric units and hospitals census 2016* (Dublin, 2016), 11.

[12] David Nowlan, 'The New Psychiatry, 1: releasing Grangegorman's 'lifers', *Irish Times,* 1 July 1985; David Nowlan, 'The New Psychiatry, 2: Making the funny farm more fun', *Irish Times,* 2 July 1985.

[13] Alan Bailey, *The Grangegorman murders: Dean Lyons, Mark Nash and the story Behind the Grangegorman murders* (Dublin, 2015).

[14] Carl O'Brien, 'Goodbye Grangegorman', *Irish Times,* 23 February 2013.

[15] Kirsten Mulrennan, 'The development of recordkeeping practices in Irish asylums: a case study of Grangegorman psychiatric hospital', in A.C. Holland and E. Mullins (eds), *Archives and archivists 2: current trends, new voices* (Dublin, 2013), 114–26.

# Bibliography

## PRIMARY SOURCES

### Manuscript

Bureau of Military History 1913–21 Collection Witness Statements. Military Archives, Cathal Brugha Barracks, Dublin:

- *Witness Statement (Number 250) of Mr William P. Corrigan* (File Number S.378).
- *Witness Statement (Number 568) of Eilís Bean Uí Chonaill* (File Number S.1846).

Committee of Management of Ballinasloe District Lunatic Asylum/ Mental Hospital 1904–1942  *Minutes of the Proceedings of the Committee of Management of Ballinasloe District Lunatic Asylum/ Mental Hospital.* Archives at St Brigid's Hospital, Ballinasloe, County Galway, Ireland.

Grangegorman Archive, *Male and Female Casebooks, Richmond War Hospital Archives (1916-1919).* National Archives of Ireland, Bishop Street, Dublin, PRIV 1223.

Grangegorman Mental Hospital 1916 *'Vegetables Issued' Book.* Dublin; Grangegorman Mental Hospital. National Archives of Ireland, PRIV 1223/22/4.

Norman, Conolly 1905–7 *Conolly Norman Lectures, Grangegorman.* Dublin. Royal College of Physicians of Ireland Heritage Centre, ACC/2017/2.

Norman, Conolly 1907 'Report of Dr Norman', in *Richmond Asylum Joint Committee Minutes.* Dublin. Richmond Asylum.

Resident Medical Superintendent 1863 *Richmond District Lunatic Asylum, Dublin: Report of the Resident Medical Superintendent for the Year 1862.* Dublin. Joseph Dollard. National Library of Ireland, Ir 3622 r1.

Resident Medical Superintendent 1863–78 *Annual Reports of the Superintendent of the Richmond District Lunatic Asylum, 1862-1877*. Dublin. Various Publishers. National Library of Ireland, Ir 3622 r1.

Richmond District Asylum 1903 *Regulations for the Management of the Richmond District Asylum under the Act 60 & 61 Victoriæ, Cap. 37*. Dublin. John Falconer. National Library of Ireland, BB4120.

Richmond Asylum Joint Committee 1907 *Richmond Asylum Joint Committee Minutes*. Dublin. Richmond Asylum.

## University theses

Grimsley-Smith, Melinda D. 2011 'Politics, professionalisation, and poverty: lunatic asylums for the poor in Ireland, 1817–1920'. PhD Thesis, University of Notre Dame, IN.

O'Brien, Eveleen 1939 'Epilepsy and its theories: results of treatment'. MD Thesis, University College Dublin.

## Printed (pre-1970)

Anonymous 1886 'Obituary: Joseph Lalor, MD', *Journal of Mental Science* 32 (139) (October), 462–3.

Anonymous 1917 'Irish Division', *Journal of Mental Science* 63 (261) (April 1917), 297–9.

Boyd Barrett, Edward 1924 'Modern psycho-therapy and our asylums', *Studies* 13 (49) (March), 29–43.

Commission of Inquiry on Mental Illness 1967 *Report of the Commission of Inquiry on Mental Illness*. Dublin. The Stationery Office.

Commission on the Relief of the Sick and Destitute Poor, Including the Insane Poor 1927 *Report of the Commission on the Relief of the Sick and Destitute Poor, Including the Insane Poor*. Dublin. The Stationery Office.

Committee on Lunacy Administration (Ireland) 1891 *First and Second Reports of the Committee Appointed by the Lord Lieutenant of Ireland on Lunacy Administration (Ireland)*. Edinburgh. Neill & Co. for Her Majesty's Stationery Office.

Dawson, William R. 1925 'The work of the Belfast War Hospital (1917–1919)', *Journal of Mental Science* 71 (293) (April), 219–24.

Duncan, James F. 1853 *Popular Errors on the Subject of Insanity: Examined and Exposed*. Dublin. James McGlashan.

Dunne, John 1926 'The malarial treatment of general paralysis', *Journal of Mental Science* 72 (298) (July), 343–6.

Dunne, John 1950 'Survey of modern physical methods of treatment for mental illness carried out in Grangegorman Mental Hospital', *Journal of the Medical Association of Eire* 27 (157) (July), 4–9.

Dunne, John 1956 'The contribution of the physical sciences to psychological medicine', *Journal of Mental Science* 102 (427) (April), 209–20.

Dunne, John and Eveleen O'Brien 1939 'Insulin therapy: a short review of the work done in Grangegorman Mental Hospital', *Journal of Mental Science* 85 (356) (May), 498–504.

Esquirol, Jean-Étienne 1805 *Des Passions*. Paris. Didot Jeune.

Fraser, James 1862 *Handbook for Dublin and its Environs including Bray and the Adjacent Parts of the County Wicklow with Map of the City and Street Maps of an Entirely New Plan (Second Edition)*. Dublin. William Robertson.

Hallaran, William S. 1810 *An Enquiry into the Causes Producing the Extraordinary Addition to the Number of Insane together with Extended Observations on the Cure of Insanity with Hints as to the Better Management of Public Asylums for Insane Persons*. Cork. Edwards and Savage.

Hallaran, William S. 1818 *Practical Observations on the Causes and Cures of Insanity (Second Edition)*. Cork. Edwards and Savage.

Inspector of Lunatic Asylums 1847 *Report on the District, Local and Private Lunatic Asylums in Ireland 1846*. Dublin. Alexander Thom, for Her Majesty's Stationery Office.

Inspectors of Lunatics (Ireland) 1893 *The Forty-Second Report (With Appendices) of the Inspectors of Lunatics (Ireland) 1892*. Dublin. Alexander Thom and Company (Limited) for Her Majesty's Stationery Office.

Inspectors of Lunatics (Ireland) 1914 *The Sixty-Third Annual Report (With Appendices) of the Inspectors of Lunatics (Ireland), Being for the Year Ending 31st December* 1913. Dublin. Thom and Co. for His Majesty's Stationery Office.

Inspectors of Lunatics (Ireland) 1917 *The Sixty-Fifth Annual Report (With Appendices) of the Inspectors of Lunatics (Ireland), Being for the Year Ending 31st December 1915*. Dublin. His Majesty's Stationery Office.

Inspector of Mental Hospitals 1930 *Annual Report of the Inspector of Mental Hospitals for the Year 1929*. Dublin. Department of Local Government and Public Health / Stationery Office.

Inspector of Mental Hospitals 1931 *Annual Report of the Inspector of Mental Hospitals for the Year 1930*. Dublin. Department of Local Government and Public Health/Stationery Office.

Inspector of Mental Hospitals 1936 *Annual Report of the Inspector of Mental Hospitals for the Year 1935*. Dublin. Department of Local Government and Public Health/Stationery Office.

Inspector of Mental Hospitals 1937 *Annual Report of the Inspector of Mental Hospitals for the Year 1936*. Dublin. Department of Local Government and Public Health/Stationery Office.

Joyce, James 1922 *Ulysses*. Franklin Centre, Pennsylvania. Franklin Library, 1976; first published in full in Paris by Sylvia Beach, 1922.

King Moylan, Thomas 1944–45 'The district of Grangegorman (Part 1)', *Dublin Historical Record* 7 (1) (December – February), 1–15.

Kirkpatrick, T. Percy C. 1931 *A Note on the History of the Care of the Insane in Ireland up to the End of the Nineteenth Century*. Dublin. University Press, Ponsonby and Gibbs.

Lalor, Joseph 1878 'On the use of education and training in the treatment of the insane in public lunatic asylums', *Journal of the Statistical and Social Inquiry of Ireland* 7 (54) (1878), 361–73.

MacGabhann, Liam 1965 'Dr Dunne retires after 45 years in St Brendan's', *Irish Times*, 31 December.

Mollan, John 1838 'Statistical report of the Richmond Lunatic Asylum', *Dublin Journal of Medical Science* 13 (3) (July), 367–84.

Myers, Charles S. 1915 'A contribution to the study of shell shock', *Lancet* 185 (4772) (13 February), 316–20.

Myers, Charles S. 1916 'Contributions to the study of shell shock: being an account of certain disorders of cutaneous sensibility', *Lancet* 187 (4829) (18 March 1916), 608–13.

Norman, Conolly 1886 'Two cases of larvated insanity', *Journal of Mental Science* 32 (137) (April), 36–44.

Norman, Conolly 1894 'Presidential address, delivered at the Royal College of Physicians, Dublin, June 12th, 1894', *Journal of Mental Science* 40 (171) (October), 487–99.

Norman, Conolly 1899 'A brief note on beri-beri in asylums', *Journal of Mental Science* 45 (190) (July), 503–12.

Norman, Conolly 1899 'The clinical features of beri-beri', *Transactions of the Royal Academy of Medicine in Ireland* 17 (1) (1 December), 145–79.

Norman, Conolly 1904 'On the need for family care of persons of unsound mind in Ireland', *Journal of Mental Science* 50 (210) (July), 461–73.

Norman, Conolly 1905 'Modern witchcraft: a study of a phase of paranoia', *Journal of Mental Science* 51 (212) (January 1905), 116–25.

O'Brien, Liam 1967 'The magic wisp: a history of the mentally ill in Ireland', *Bulletin of the Menninger Clinic* 31 (2) (March), 79–95.

O'Neill, Edward D. 1903 *Increase of Lunacy and Special Reasons Applicable to Ireland.* Limerick: George McKern and Sons Limited.

O'Sullivan, Eamon N.M. 1955 *Textbook of Occupational Therapy with Chief Reference to Psychological Medicine.* London. H.K Lewis and Co. Ltd.

Phillips, Norman R. 1938 'Daniel Frederick Rambaut', *Journal of Mental Science* 84 (348) (January), 1–2.

Redington, J.M. and P.J. Dwyer 1909 'Maniacal-depressive insanity amongst the male admissions to the Richmond District Asylum in the year 1907', *Journal of Mental Science* 55 (228) (January), 56–8.

Select Committee of the House of Lords 1843 *Report from the Select Committee of the House of Lords Appointed to Consider the State of the Lunatic Poor in Ireland and to Report Thereon to the House with the Minutes of Evidence, Appendix, and Index.* London. House of Commons.

Select Committee on the Lunatic Poor in Ireland 1817 *Report from the Select Committee on the Lunatic Poor in Ireland with Minutes of Evidence Taken Before the Committee and an Appendix.* London. House of Commons.

Select Committee on Lunatic Asylums (Ireland) (Advances) Bill 1855 *Minutes of Evidence.* London. House of Commons.

Stoker, Bram 1897 *Dracula* London. Archibald Constable and Company.

Tuke, Daniel H. 1875 'On the Richmond Asylum schools', *Journal of Mental Science* 21 (95) (October), 467–74.

## Newspapers

*Building News and Engineering Journal*
*Evening Herald*
*Freeman's Journal*
*Irish Independent*
*Irish Press*
*Irish Times*
*Manchester Guardian*
*Weekly Irish Times*

## SECONDARY SOURCES (1970 ONWARDS)

Bailey, Alan 2015 *The Grangegorman murders: Dean Lyons, Mark Nash and the story behind the Grangegorman murders.* Dublin. Gill and Macmillan.

Brennan, Damien 2014 *Irish insanity, 1800–2000.* Abingdon, Oxon. Routledge.

Browne, Ivor 2008 *Music and madness.* Cork. Atrium/Cork University Press.

Cherry, Steven and Roger Munting 2005 '"Exercise is the thing"? Sport and the asylum *c.* 1850–1950', *International Journal of the History of Sport* 22 (1), 42–58.

Collins, Aidan 2007 *St Vincent's Hospital, Fairview: an illustrated history, 1857–2007.* Dublin. Albertine Kennedy Publishing with Duke Kennedy Sweetman.

Collins, Aidan 2013 'Eleonora Fleury captured', *British Journal of Psychiatry* 203 (1) (July), 5.

Collins, Aidan 2013 'The Richmond District Asylum and the 1916 Easter Rising', *Irish Journal of Psychological Medicine* 30 (4) (December), 279–83.

Collins, Aidan 2014 'Fleury, Eleonora Lilian', in J. McGuire and J. Quinn (eds), *Dictionary of Irish Biography*. Cambridge. Cambridge University Press.

Collins, Aidan 2017 'Daniel Frederick Rambaut: "Rugbanian" and innovative resident medical superintendent', *Irish Journal of Psychological Medicine* 34 (1) (March), 75–8.

Cox, Catherine 2012 *Negotiating Insanity in the southeast of Ireland, 1820–1900*. Manchester and New York. Manchester University Press.

Crawford, E. Margaret 2012 'A mysterious malady in an Irish asylum: the Richmond epidemic of the late nineteenth century', in P.M. Prior (ed.), *Asylums, Mental Health Care and the Irish, 1800–2010*, 185–204. Dublin and Portland, OR. Irish Academic Press.

Daly, Antoinette and Sarah Craig 2016 *Irish psychiatric units and hospitals census 2016*. Dublin, Health Research Board.

Dunne, Bríd D., Katie Robinson and Judith Pettigrew 2018 'A case study of the development of occupational therapy at St. Patrick's Hospital Dublin, 1935–1969', *Irish Journal of Occupational Therapy* 46 (1), 31–45.

Finnane, Mark 1981 *Insanity and the insane in post-Famine Ireland*. London. Croom Helm.

FitzGerald, Garret 2013 *Irish primary education in the early nineteenth century: an analysis of the First and Second Reports of the Commissioners of Irish Education Inquiry, 1825–6*. Dublin. Royal Irish Academy.

Fogarty, Weeshie 2007 *Dr Eamonn O'Sullivan: a man before his time*. Dublin. Wolfhound Press.

Henry, Hanora M. 1989 *Our Lady's Psychiatric Hospital Cork*. Cork. Haven Books.

Kelly, Brendan D. 2005 'Physical sciences and psychological medicine: the legacy of Prof John Dunne'. *Irish Journal of Psychological Medicine* 22 (2) (June), 67–72.

Kelly, Brendan D. 2007 'One hundred years ago: the Richmond Asylum, Dublin in 1907', *Irish Journal of Psychological Medicine* 24 (3) (September), 108–14.

Kelly, Brendan D. 2008 'Dr William Saunders Hallaran and psychiatric practice in nineteenth-century Ireland', *Irish Journal of Medical Science* 177 (1) (March), 79–84.

Kelly, Brendan D. 2012 'Tuberculosis in the nineteenth-century asylum: clinical cases from the Central Criminal Lunatic Asylum, Dundrum, Dublin', in P.M. Prior (ed.) *Asylums, Mental Health Care and the Irish, 1800–2010*, 205–20. Dublin and Portland, OR. Irish Academic Press.

Kelly, Brendan D. 2014 *Ada English: patriot and psychiatrist*. Sallins, County Kildare. Irish Academic Press.

Kelly, Brendan D. 2014 *'He lost himself completely': shell shock and its treatment at Dublin's Richmond War Hospital, 1916–1919*. Dublin. Liffey Press.

Kelly, Brendan D. 2015 'Shell shock in Ireland: the Richmond War Hospital, Dublin (1916–19)', *History of Psychiatry* 26 (1) (March), 50–63.

Kelly, Brendan D. 2016 *Hearing voices: the history of psychiatry in Ireland*. Dublin. Irish Academic Press.

Kelly, Brendan D. 2017 'Ego, id and Ireland', *Lancet Psychiatry* 4 (4) (April), 281–2.

Kelly, Brendan D. 2017 'Dr Dermot Walsh, 1931–2017', *Irish Journal of Psychological Medicine* 34 (3) (September), 217–20.

Kelly, Brendan D. 2019 'The Great Irish Famine (1845–52) and the Irish asylum system: remembering, forgetting, and remembering again', *Irish Journal of Medical Science* 188 (3) (August), 953–8.

Kelly, Niamh A. 2018 *Imaging the Great Irish Famine: representing dispossession in visual culture*. London. I.B. Tauris.

Malcolm, Elizabeth 1989 *Swift's Hospital: a history of St Patrick's Hospital, Dublin, 1746–1989*. Dublin. Gill and Macmillan.

Mauger, Alice 2012 '"Confinement of the higher orders": The social role of private lunatic asylums in Ireland, *c.* 1820–60', *Journal of the History of Medicine and Allied Sciences* 67 (2) (April), 281–317.

Mauger, Alice 2018 *The cost of insanity in nineteenth-century Ireland: public, voluntary and private asylum care.* Cham. Palgrave Macmillan.

McCabe, Anton and Ciaran Mulholland 2012 'The red flag over the asylum', in P.M. Prior (ed.), *Asylums, mental health care and the Irish, 1800–2010,* 23–43. Dublin and Portland, Oregon. Irish Academic Press.

Mulrennan, Kirsten 2013 'The development of recordkeeping practices in Irish asylums: a case study of Grangegorman Psychiatric Hospital', in A.C. Holland and E. Mullins (eds), *Archives and Archivists 2: current trends, new voices,* 114–26. Dublin. Four Courts Press.

Nowlan, David 1985 'The New Psychiatry, 1: Releasing Grangegorman's 'lifers', *Irish Times,* 1 July.

Nowlan, David 1985 'The New Psychiatry, 2: Making the funny farm more fun', *Irish Times,* 2 July.

O'Brien, Carl 2013 'Goodbye Grangegorman', *Irish Times,* 23 February.

O'Callaghan, Aoife K. and Brendan D. Kelly 2019 'Dr Eveleen O'Brien (1901–1981)', *Irish Journal of Medical Science* 188 (2) 649–52.

O'Shea, Brian and Jane Falvey 1996 'A history of the Richmond Asylum (St Brendan's Hospital), Dublin', in H. Freeman and G.E. Berrios (eds), *150 years of British psychiatry. Volume II: The aftermath,* 407–33. London. Athlone Press.

Prendiville, Caren and Judith Pettigrew 2015 'Leisure occupations in the Central Criminal Lunatic Asylum 1890–1920', *Irish Journal of Occupational Therapy* 43 (1) (Spring), 12–9.

Prior, Pauline M. 2008 *Madness and murder: gender, crime and mental disorder in nineteenth century Ireland.* Dublin and Portland, OR. Irish Academic Press.

Reynolds, Joseph 1992 *Grangegorman: psychiatric care in Dublin since 1815.* Dublin. Institute of Public Administration in association with Eastern Health Board.

Robins, Joseph 1986 *Fools and mad: a history of the insane in Ireland.* Dublin. Institute of Public Administration.

Robins, Joseph 2000 *Nursing and midwifery in Ireland in the twentieth century*. Dublin. An Bord Altranais.

Shephard, Ben 2002 *A war of nerves: soldiers and psychiatrists, 1914–1994*. London. Pimlico.

Sheridan, Ann J. 2006 'The impact of political transition on psychiatric nursing: a case study of twentieth-century Ireland', *Nursing Inquiry* 13 (4), 289–99.

Walsh, Dermot 2012 'Did the Great Irish Famine increase schizophrenia?', *Irish Journal of Psychological Medicine* 29 (1) (January), 7–15.

Walsh, Dermot and Antoinette Daly 2004 *Mental illness in Ireland 1750–2002: reflections on the rise and fall of institutional care*. Dublin. Health Research Board.

Walsh, Oonagh 2004 'Gender and insanity in nineteenth-century Ireland', in J. Andrews and A. Digby (eds), *Sex and seclusion, class and custody: perspectives on gender and class in the history of British and Irish psychiatry*. Amsterdam. Editions Rodopi, 69–93.

Walsh, Oonagh 2012 'A perfectly ordered establishment: Connaught District Lunatic Asylum (Ballinasloe)', in P.M. Prior (ed.), *Asylums, mental health care and the Irish, 1800–2010*, 246–70. Dublin and Portland, OR. Irish Academic Press.

Walsh, Oonagh 2016 '"An invisible but inescapable trauma": epigenetics and the Great Famine', in C. Kinealy, J. King and C. Reilly (eds), *Women and the Great Hunger*, 173–83. Hamden, CT. Quinnipiac University Press.

Walsh, Tom 2016 'The national system of education, 1831–2000', in B. Walsh (ed), *Essays in the history of Irish education*, 7–43. London. Palgrave Macmillan.

# Profiles

### Richard Grace, Moral Governor, 1816–30

Richard Grace was appointed first Moral Governor (manager) of the Richmond Asylum on 1 February 1816, two years after it opened. Two years later, Grace advised the governors that the institution was already overcrowded. There was a risk, he warned, that 'the original objects of the institution will be frustrated and it will be converted from a curative asylum into a depot of incurables'. Grace's wife, Ann, was appointed matron and housekeeper but died in 1821. Ann was replaced by Grace's sister, Philippa, who brought renewed enthusiasm to the running of the asylum. Grace died in office in 1830.

### Dr William Heisse, Asylum Manager, 1830–31

Dr William Heisse was manager of the Richmond District Lunatic Asylum from September 1830 to June 1831. Heisse had served with the British army in the Peninsular War and, from 1808, practised medicine in Borrisokane, County Tipperary. He was appointed to the Richmond in September 1830 but just ten months later, in June 1831, the inspectors reported that the asylum was in a dirty condition and that restraints were being used without proper recording. These complaints, although serious, were not new. Nonetheless, Heisse was abruptly dismissed by the Lord Lieutenant, much to Heisse's dismay. Heisse had, as he wrote to the governors, 'a large family of a wife and nine children wholly depending on me'. The governors protested at the Lord Lieutenant's decision and provided Heisse with a favourable testimonial, but they were powerless: the asylum was a highly politicised place and, for reasons that were never made clear, the Lord Lieutenant wanted Heisse out.

### Samuel Wrigley, Moral Governor, 1831–57

Appointed in July 1831 following the abrupt dismissal of Dr William Heisse, Samuel Wrigley served as moral governor of the Richmond

District Lunatic Asylum from 1831 to 1857, with his wife as matron. Prior to his appointment to the Richmond, Wrigley was superintendent in the Dublin House of Industry. Wrigley was a firm manager who initially brought a new level of rigour and efficiency to the Richmond. He was especially keen that patients should be gainfully occupied making clothing and bedding for the asylum and working on the buildings or grounds. Over the course of Wrigley's 26 years at the asylum, the Richmond became known as 'Wrigley's' or, later, 'Ridley's'. During the 1850s, however, the state of the asylum again declined and, following exhaustive enquiries, it was decided that the establishment should be run by a doctor in future. Somewhat harshly, both Wrigley and his wife were dismissed in November 1857.

## Dr Joseph Lalor, Resident Medical Superintendent, 1857-86

Dr Joseph Lalor, who served as Resident Medical Superintendent from 1857 to 1886, paid particular attention to the Richmond school, considering education to be the fundamental basis of moral treatment of the insane. In 1861, Lalor became the eighth president, and first Irish president, of the Medico Psychological Association, fore-runner of the Royal College of Psychiatrists. Notwithstanding this eminence—or possibly because of it—Lalor had a deeply complicated relationship with the asylum governors who excluded him from meetings in the 1870s. He had an even more conflictual relationship with the Inspector, Dr John Nugent, who was unusually involved in asylum management. All of this led to an enquiry, in 1883, which clearly vindicated Lalor. Following his death in 1886, the *Journal of Mental Science* paid tribute to Lalor's undoubted achievements at the Richmond.

## Dr Conolly Norman, Resident Medical Superintendent, 1886-1908

The leading psychiatrist of his generation, Conolly Norman was born in 1853 in Donegal and educated at Trinity College Dublin, the Carmichael School of Medicine (North Brunswick Street) and the

Richmond Hospital. Norman worked as assistant medical officer at Monaghan District Asylum from 1874 to 1881, then at Bethlem Royal Hospital in London, before becoming medical superintendent at district asylums in Castlebar (1882–5) and Monaghan (1885–6).

Appointed to the Richmond in 1886, Norman was especially enthusiastic about patients 'boarding out' of the asylum, and 'family care of persons of unsound mind'. He noted that there were many objections to be made against asylum life, not least of which was its separation of patients from the ordinary interests of life. Norman was deeply opposed to prolonged asylum admission but his efforts to create alternatives were repeatedly frustrated by a government and society with unending desires for institutionalisation.

Norman's gargantuan efforts to improve care at the Richmond took a toll on his health, but he persisted with a heavy workload and many additional interests: book collecting, literature, botany, archaeology, architecture, music and languages (German, French, Italian). In 1894, Norman became president of the Medico Psychological Association, an honour he richly merited. Norman was a prominent pubic figure and was mentioned by James Joyce in 'Ulysses'. Norman died in office in 1908 and is commemorated in St Patrick's Cathedral, Dublin.

## Dr John O'Conor Donelan, Resident Medical Superintendent, 1908–37

Dr John O'Conor Donelan served as Resident Medical Superintendent from 1908 to 1937. He oversaw significant changes at the Richmond including its increased politicisation during Ireland's revolutionary years (1912–1923) and the establishment of the Richmond War Hospital, which treated 362 soldiers with shell shock and various other mental problems between June 1916 and December 1919. Most of all, O'Conor Donelan oversaw structural improvements to the main asylum: new wards and infirmaries built, high walls removed, and enclosed yards converted to brighter recreation grounds. Even these measures, however, could not relieve conditions in the institution, as around 100 patients were transferred from various workhouses to the Richmond each year, resulting in continued overcrowding. O'Conor Donelan retired in 1937, at the age of 70.

## Professor John Dunne, Chief Resident Medical Superintendent, 1937–65

Professor John Dunne served as Chief Resident Medical Superintendent from 1937 to 1965. An iconic figure in Irish asylum medicine, Dunne introduced malaria therapy at Grangegorman in the mid-1920s when he was Assistant Medical Officer. As Chief Resident Medical Superintendent, he introduced and studied all the novel physical treatments of the era including insulin coma, lobotomy, convulsive therapy (especially electro-convulsive therapy or ECT) and anti-psychotic medication. He was appointed professor of psychiatry at University College Dublin in 1950. Dunne also introduced better living and sleeping conditions for patients in Grangegorman, enhanced the library facilities, promoted the appointment of social workers, and led the formation of an after-care committee for discharged patients. Most of all, Dunne managed to finally reduce patient numbers in Grangegorman, from over 2,000 when he took up his position in 1937, to approximately 700 when he retired from St Brendan's Hospital (as it was then called) in 1965. A keen sportsman, Dunne died in 1991 at the age of 92.

## Professor Ivor Browne, Chief Psychiatrist, 1965–1994

Professor Ivor Browne served as chief psychiatrist at St Brendan's Hospital from 1965 to 1994 and professor of psychiatry at University College Dublin from 1967 to 1994. Browne pioneered novel and, at times, unorthodox treatments at St Brendan's. He led the further dismantling of the old institution and the development of community mental health services during the 1970s and 1980s. He established the Irish Foundation for Human Development (1968–79) and, in 1983, was appointed chairman of the group of European experts set up by the European Economic Community for the reform of Greek psychiatry. After his retirement in 1994, Browne continued clinical work and pursued his interests in stress management, living system theory, how the brain processes traumatic experiences, and the Sahag Marg system of meditation.

# Acknowledgements

Many people assisted and advised me as I wrote this book. I am deeply indebted to all the colleagues and friends who answered my emails and calls, and discussed various themes with me as the project progressed.

I am especially grateful to Ruth Hegarty, Valeria Cavalli and staff at the Royal Irish Academy; Catriona Crowe; Kirsten Mulrennan; Brian Donnelly, Deirdre O'Connell and the staff at the National Archives of Ireland; Dr Larkin Feeney; Dr Aidan Collins; Dr John Bruzzi; Professor John Kelly; Professor Veronica O'Keane; Alison Collie; Elizabeth Kehoe and Terry Crosbie (Stoneybatter & Smithfield People's History Project); Anne O'Connor, Danny Connellan, Seán Tone and Carmel Kitching (Health Service Executive); and Harriet Wheelock (Heritage Centre, Royal College of Physicians of Ireland).

I owe a long-standing debt of gratitude to my teachers at Scoil Chaitríona, Renmore, Galway; St Joseph's Patrician College, Nun's Island, Galway (especially my history teacher, Ciaran Doyle); and the School of Medicine at NUI Galway.

Finally, and above all else, I deeply appreciate the support of my wife, Regina, and children, Eoin and Isabel. I am also very grateful to my parents (Mary and Desmond), sisters (Sinéad and Niamh) and nieces (Aoife and Aisling). And, of course, Trixie deserves special mention: we miss you.

## Permissions

I am very grateful to a range of editors, publishers, authors and copyright-holders for permitting re-use of material in this book. All reasonable efforts have been made to contact the copyright holders for all texts quoted and images used. If any have been omitted, please contact the publisher.

# Index

# G

Galway gaol, 113
general hospitals, 12–13, 58, 71,
    130, 137
general paralysis of the insane
    (GPI), 123
Grace, Richard, 23, 167
Great Famine (1845–52), 51–2
grounds, 17, 26, 32

# H

Hallaran, William Saunders, 5, 23–4
hallucinations *see* noises; visions;
    voices
Hartfield House asylum,
    Drumcondra, 75
Head Attendant, 84–5
Head Nurse, 83–4
headaches, 40, 95, 101, 102, 103,
    104, 105
heart disease, 43, 53–4, 57, 58, 62, 65
Heisse, William, 23, 167
Hermitage Hospital, Lucan, 97
homelessness, 138
Homerton Fever Hospital, London,
    112
hospitals *see* general hospitals; war
    hospitals
Howard, George, 7th Earl of
    Carlisle, 4
hydro-therapy, 28
hygiene, 34, 57, 58, 63–4, 139

# I

'incurables', 6, 8, 34, 46, 63, 118
industrial relations, 90–1, 117

industrial therapies, 30
insanity, recorded causes of, 5, 32,
    56
insomnia, 97, 102, 103, 104
Inspectors of Lunatics, 8–9, 51,
    100, 105, 117
Inspectors of Mental Hospitals,
    79, 85
insulin therapy, 120, 123–4, 129, 135
intellectual disabilities, 3, 8–9, 17,
    38, 55, 78, 83, 110
Irish Automobile Club, 100
Irish Free State, 79
Irish Psycho-Analytical
    Association, 130

# J

Jackson, Alexander, 26, 82
Joint Committee, Richmond
    District Asylum 12, 45, 52,
    111–12, 114–18
*Journal of Mental Science*, 48, 105

# K

Kearney, Joseph, 85
Kelly, Daniel L., 79
Kilkenny Mental Hospital, 85
Killarney Mental Hospital, 30
King George V Hospital, 97

# L

Lalor, Joseph, 47–8, 82, 168
*Lancet*, 95
laundry, 16, 26, 84
leisure activities *see* recreation

paralysis, 29, 63, 65, 123
paranoia, 31, 58
Peace Commissioners, 117
Phoenix Care Centre, 139
phthisis see tuberculosis
pneumonia, 9, 63, 103, 106, 123
police, 3, 31, 39, 71, 74, 87–8
Portrane asylum, 12, 18, 29, 31, 55, 62, 64, 71, 77, 111, 112, 116
post-mortems, 65, 122
poverty, 38, 47, 87, 122, 315
prisons, 3–4, 7–8, 12–13, 71, 73–4, 113, 130, 138
private asylums, 8, 38, 75
Property Losses (Ireland) Committee, 88
psychoanalysis, 130–1

## Q

quinine, 101, 123

## R

Radcliffe War Hospital, 101
Rambaut, Daniel Frederick, 11–12, 48, 54–5
recovery, 6, 17, 25–6, 28, 40, 42, 52, 63, 70, 73, 102, 105–6
recreation, 30, 47, 100, 106
Redington, J.M., 75
Redmond, John, 114
regulations, 43–5, 52–3, 83–6
rehabilitation, 129
religion, 5, 8, 29, 32–3, 51, 56, 69, 130
residential units, 137, 138
restlessness, 11, 13, 14, 16, 17, 37, 40, 52, 60, 66, 67, 104–5

restraint, 23, 36, 44
Richmond War Hospital, 94–107
Royal College of Surgeons in Ireland, 54
Royal Hospital for the Incurables, 134
Royal University of Ireland, 112

## S

St Bricin's Hospital see King George V Hospital
St Brigid's Mental Hospital, Ballinasloe, 30, 113–14
St Loman's Hospital, Dublin, 137
St Patrick's Hospital, Dublin, 8, 30
Sakel, Manfred, 123
schizophrenia, 51, 124, 125
school, 47–8, 82
shell shock, 94–9
shower-baths, 28
Sinn Féin, 113, 115
sedation, 23
seizures, 123, 125–8
self-harm, 50, 64
sleep, 46, 99, 101, 102, 103, 104–5, 106; see also dreams; insomnia
sleeping facilities, 44, 129
Sneyd, Nathaniel, 2–3
social class, 7
social workers, 129
Somme, Battle of the (1916), 94–5
South Dublin Union, 29
sport, 30, 48, 100; see also exercise
staff, 44–5, 48, 54, 82–6, 90–1, 96, 118, 139
staff training, 83, 85, 91
Stoker, Bram, 54
Stoker, William Thornley, 54